P9-EMP-067

SIERRA LEONE

Suzanne LeVert

Marshall Cavendish
Benchmark
New York

PICTURE CREDITS

Cover photo: © Karl Kummels/SuperStock

alt.TYPE/REUTERS: 14, 31, 38, 39, 42, 94, 111, 113, 126 • Corbis Inc.: 24, 26, 28, 34, 53, 65, 69, 84, 89, 98, 101, 110, 118, 121, 124, 127 • FoodPhotogr. Eising/Stockfood: 131 • Juliet Highet/Hutchison Library: 120 • Hutchison Library: 104, 116, 122 • Karl Kummels/SuperStock: 68 • R Ian Lloyd/nevio doz: 12 • R Ian Lloyd/SuperStock: 64 • Lonely Planet Images: 8, 72 • Marshall Cavendish International (Asia): 130 • Panos Pictures: 1, 4, 5, 6, 17, 19, 3, 32, 33, 36, 37, 40, 44, 46, 49, 51, 54, 55, 56, 57, 60, 62, 66, 75, 76, 78, 80, 82, 83, 86, 87, 90, 91, 92, 97, 102, 105, 106, 108, 112, 114, 115, 128 • Photolibrary: 20 58 • www.tropix.co.uk: 11, 63, 71, 100, 129

PRECEDING PAGE

Sierra Leoneans gather with family and friends on Lumley Beach in the capital, Freetown, on Easter Sunday.

Marshall Cavendish Benchmark
99 White Plains Road
Tarrytown, NY 10591
Website: www.marshallcavendish.us

© Marshall Cavendish International (Asia) Private Limited 2006
® "Cultures of the World" is a registered trademark of Marshall Cavendish Corporation.

Series concept and design by Times Editions
An imprint of Marshall Cavendish International (Asia) Private Limited
A member of Times Publishing Limited

Library of Congress Cataloging-in-Publication Data
LeVert, Suzanne.
    Sierra Leone / by Suzanne LeVert.—1st ed.
       p. cm. — (Cultures of the world)
    Summary: "Provides comprehensive information on the geography, history, governmental structure,
       economy, cultural diversity, peoples, religion, and culture of Sierra Leone"—Provided by publisher.
    Includes bibliographical references and index.
    ISBN-13: 978-0-7614-2334-8
    ISBN-10: 0-7614-2334-6
    1. Sierra Leone—Juvenile literature. I. Title. II. Series.
    DT516.18.L48 2007
    966.4—dc22   2005035964

Printed in China

7 6 5 4 3 2 1

CONTENTS

A young girl carries firewood.

An advertisement for a mobile telephone company in Sierra Leone.

INTRODUCTION

EMBROILED IN CORRUPTION and internal strife since gaining independence in 1961, the West African country of Sierra Leone only recently ended a decades-long civil war. More than 500,000 people fled the country during the war and are only slowly making their way home. Hundreds of thousands of men, women, and children suffer from medical and psychological problems stemming from their experience of the war. They face an already overburdened and underfinanced health care system. Sierra Leone's president, Ahmad Tejan Kabbah, has been working with international peacekeeping forces and humanitarian aid organizations since 2002 to rebuild the country's infrastructure and to heal the people's social, economic, and psychological wounds. The country's vast harbor, rich mineral deposits, and stunning beaches and forests are some of the natural resources ready to be tapped to support the 6 million people who call Sierra Leone home.

GEOGRAPHY

SIERRA LEONE IS SITUATED on the western coast of Africa. It shares borders with two countries: Guinea to the north and east and Liberia to the south. Its western border is a 210-mile (340-km) coastline on the Atlantic Ocean. Lying between the 7th and 10th parallels north of the equator, Sierra Leone is roughly circular in shape and covers approximately 27,900 square miles (71,749 square km). It is slightly smaller than South Carolina. Its name, given by Portuguese explorers in the 15th century purportedly because of its wild terrain, means "Lion Mountain." Sierra Leone's territory includes several offshore islands, including Sherbro, Banana, and Bunce.

Sierra Leone has four main geographic areas: the Interior Plateaus and Mountains Region, the Interior Low Plains Region, the Coastal Swampland Region, and the Freetown Peninsula.

The Interior Plateaus and Mountains Region consists of a large area of plateaus dotted with larger mountain peaks. This region of eastern Sierra Leone contains the country's highest point: Mount Bintumani (also called Loma Mansa), at 6,381 feet (1,945 m). In this region's southern section lies the upper basin of the Moa River. The Interior Low Plains Region stretches from the interior plateaus and mountains to the coastal swamps. Most of this region is made up of forest, farmland, and bush.

The Coastal Swampland Region is filled with estuaries—waterways that form where the ocean tide meets a river current. It also contains swamps teeming with mangrove trees that are common along tropical coasts. The Freetown Peninsula is about 25 miles (40 km) long and 10 miles (16 km) wide. A hilly area with peaks rising as high as 3,280 feet (1,000 m), this region contains a forest reserve as well as several beaches. The city of Freetown and other large towns are located just above these beaches.

Opposite: **Coastal flora and misty mountains on the Freetown Peninsula.**

Administratively, Sierra Leone is divided into four areas: the Central, Northern, and Southern provinces and the Western Area, which includes the capital, Freetown. Each of these areas is further divided into districts, which are then divided into chiefdoms according to ethnic and patrilineal lines. Currently, there are 149 chiefdoms in Sierra Leone.

CLIMATE AND SEASONS

Residents of the northern town of Kabala have had to adapt to the heat and dust of the region.

Sierra Leone is a tropical country blanketed with heat and humidity for much of the year. During the rainy season, humidity is as high as 90 percent early in the morning, although it can drop to about 50 percent

in some regions at night. The temperature hovers between about 80°F (26°C) and 90°F (36°C) throughout the year.

Sierra Leone has two main seasons. The dry season lasts from December to April, when dry winds from the Sahara desert blow sand over much of the country. These winds, called harmattan, are nicknamed "the Doctor" because of the healthful benefits they are supposed to have. The particles of dust carried by the harmattan produce a yellowish-white haze that blurs the horizon. Less than 3 inches (7.6 cm) of rain falls in most areas of Sierra Leone during the dry season. This contrasts sharply with the rainy season, which brings more than 120 inches (300 cm) of rain throughout the country.

The rainy season lasts from May to December. This is the time for farmers in rural areas to plant seeds of millet, cassava, and rice, as well as a variety of vegetables, including beans, tomatoes, and peppers. The heavy rains often cause flooding. In August 2005, for instance, torrential rains killed at least 20 people and destroyed hundreds of homes in the Pujehun District, which lies about 185 miles (300 km) south of Freetown. A team of rescue workers from the Sierra Leone army, the Red Cross, and the United Nations Mission in Sierra Leone (UNAMSIL) attempted to rescue more than 15,000 people stranded in flooded villages.

ISLANDS

Sierra Leone's largest island is Sherbro. Lying to the southeast of Freetown, Sherbro Island consists of the town of Bonthe and a number of little islands that form an archipelago. Other important Sherbro centers are Bendu, Victoria, and York Island.

European ships began stopping at Sherbro Island in the early 17th century to buy ivory, which was in plentiful supply, and to establish trading posts. Trade in palm products surpassed trade in all other goods. Today, Bonthe remains an important port of Sierra Leone. As part of its redevelopment plan following the civil war, the government is now building a new international airport on Sherbro Island.

The Banana Islands are located just off the southern tip of the Freetown Peninsula. Near Dublin Village in the northern part of the island are ruins of a church and a slave center built by some of the first Portuguese explorers. The remains of what probably were a slave ship and about 20 cannons still litter the seabed about 15 feet (4.6 m) beneath the water's surface along the shore. The beaches that surround the Banana Islands are perfect for diving and snorkeling. There are hundreds of fish and several different species of coral to view. Pods of whales live in deeper waters farther offshore.

Founded around 1670, Bunce Island was the largest British slave-trading post in West Africa. Located in the Sierra Leone River about 20 miles (32 km) north of modern Freetown, Bunce Island is now a national historic site under the protection of the National Tourist Board of Sierra Leone and the Monuments and Relics Commission. There are substantial ruins on the island, including a factory house, a fortification, a slave prison, watchtowers, dormitories, and storerooms.

Bunce Island has several interesting ties to the United States. During the 1750s, the island's principal owner, Richard Oswald, forged a strong relationship with Henry Laurens, one of the richest rice planters and slave dealers in the colony of South Carolina. Rice planters in coastal South Carolina and Georgia were willing to pay high prices for people brought from the Rice Coast of West Africa, where farmers were experts at the cultivation of rice. During the American Revolution in 1779, the French allied with the Americans. Jealous of the British commercial success on

Bunce Island, they attacked and destroyed the settlement. Many African Americans now living in the coastal regions of South Carolina and Georgia are descendants of slaves who had been brought to the United States from Bunce Island. Called the Gullah, they speak a Creole language similar to that spoken by the Krio community in Sierra Leone.

RIVERS, LAKES, AND MOUNTAINS

There are nine main river systems evenly distributed throughout Sierra Leone. In general, they flow from the mountains in the northeast to the coastal lowlands in the southwest and finally to the Atlantic Ocean. Most of the rivers are navigable for only a few miles at a time before they are

The densely forested banks of the Moa River.

blocked by rapids, waterfalls, and sandbanks. The rivers also become difficult to navigate when flooding occurs in the rainy season. Nevertheless, many Sierra Leoneans use small boats to travel from village to village, and the rivers provide drinking water for much of the rural population.

Two of Sierra Leone's largest rivers flow to the Atlantic Ocean. The Great Scarcies, also known as the Kolenten River, makes up part of the boundary with Guinea. The Mano River forms part of the border with Liberia. Another important waterway is the Niger River. Its headwaters are in the mountains of the northeast.

Many of Sierra Leone's rivers contain waterfalls and rapids. Charlotte Falls is located close to the Takudama Reservoir, a beautiful area located in a valley between two large hills just north of Freetown. Although smaller in size, the Sierra Leone River contains the country's two main harbors, Freetown Harbor and the port at the town of Pepel. Formed

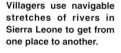

Villagers use navigable stretches of rivers in Sierra Leone to get from one place to another.

by the Rokel River and the Port Loko Creek in western Sierra Leone, the Sierra Leone River is just 25 miles (40 km) long and between 4 and 120 miles (6 and 16 km) wide.

Sierra Leone's northeastern border is filled with mountain ranges from which many of its rivers flow. These ranges include the Kangari Hills, the Tingi Hills, and the Loma Mountains. Mount Bintumani, Sierra Leone's highest point, is located in the Loma Mountains, a range that extends about 20 miles (32 km) in a north-south direction west of the Niger River. In the southeast, near the town of Kenema, lie the Kambui Hills, where the majority of the country's valuable stores of diamonds are found. The Gola Hills are the site of the Gola Forest Reserve, where the country's last significant rain forest is preserved.

FLORA

Sierra Leone is teeming with trees and vegetation. In fact, the country was once largely covered by evergreen and deciduous rain forests. Many of these forest areas have been lost through commercial logging, farming, and cattle grazing. Today only 15 percent of Sierra Leone's land is covered by forests.

There are two different kinds of rain forest in Sierra Leone: tropical rain forest and moist semi-deciduous rain forest. Found mainly in forest reserves in the Eastern Province and the Western Area, the tropical rain forest is characterized by trees that bear drip-tip leaves. The long and narrow shape of these leaves allows moisture to flow quickly off the surface of the leaves. The trees in the semi-deciduous rain forest drop their leaves during the drier months. The rain forests of Sierra Leone contain valuable timber trees, such as African oak or teak, rosewood, ebony, tamarind, camwood, and odum.

The coastline, creeks, and lower courses of the rivers, on the other hand, are lined with mangrove trees. The mangrove sends down roots from its branches and grows over water. If left to grow, it will reach a height of more than 100 feet (30 m). Large areas of the coastal regions are covered with brushwood and scattered with baobab, shea-butter, bread fruit, corkwood, and silk-cotton trees. The characteristic tree of the coastal districts is the oil palm, which is the source of Sierra Leoneans' prime cooking oil. Oil is obtained from other trees and shrubs as well, including the *benni* oil plant.

Sierra Leone also has its share of dye-yielding shrubs and plants, such as camwood and indigo. Gum is obtained from the copal, acacia, and African tragacanth plants. The blood plum, a crimson-colored fruit that grows in grapelike clusters, is one of the many kinds of fruit that grow in Sierra Leone. The Sierra Leone peach is a common crop. Before the civil war disrupted cultivation, coffee and cotton formed an important sector of Sierra Leone's export economy. Ferns are abundant in the marshes.

A baby chimpanzee at the Tacugama Chimp Sanctuary. Newcomers are quarantined to prevent the spread of disease. They are released after a few months to live with the other chimpanzees in the sanctuary.

FAUNA

Although antelopes, buffaloes, and hippopotamuses were once common in Sierra Leone, their numbers are now relatively small due to overhunting. Nevertheless, Sierra Leone is home to a host of animals, including the elephant (still found in large numbers), the leopard and panther, the chimpanzee and grey monkey, the wild hog, the bush goat and bush pig, the sloth, the civet, and the squirrel. In the southeast, a few hours

CHIMPANZEES GALORE!

Located about a 30-minute drive north of Freetown, the Tacugama Chimp Sanctuary was established in 1995 to rescue and rehabilitate orphaned chimpanzees. About 100 acres (40 ha) of semi-wild reserve is set aside for this refuge.

At one time, more than 20,000 wild chimpanzees lived in Sierra Leone. Since the 1970s, the population of chimpanzees has declined dramatically. Today there are fewer than 3,000. The reasons for the decline here, as well as in other African countries, include the use of chimpanzees for food, and the spread of human habitat and activity. The international demand for chimpanzees for use in research laboratories has also taken a toll on the population.

The Tacugama Chimp Sanctuary came to life in 1988, when Bala Amarasekeran and his wife, Shamila, saw a baby chimpanzee being offered for sale on the side of the road near Freetown. The chimpanzee looked sick and weak, and Bala and Sharmila decided to buy it and nurse it back to health. Soon, word of that deed and of the couple's willingness to help other abandoned or abused chimpanzees spread throughout the country.

Today 68 chimpanzees live in the sanctuary. The sanctuary ensures that the species will survive, at least as long as this haven has people like the Amarasekerans and their supporters looking after them.

away from the country's diamond-mining capital, Kenema, is the Tiwai Island Wildlife Sanctuary, home to more than 11 types of primates, and 135 types of birds.

Sierra Leonean skies are filled with birds of several different species, including hawks, parrots, owls, woodpeckers, kingfishers, green pigeons, and canaries. Among the more colorful species are the hornbill and the touraco. In Sierra Leone, the main type of touraco has violet-colored feathers and feasts on plantains as a mainstay of its diet. Bird lovers have recorded more than 626 bird species in Sierra Leone, of which more than 430 are resident species and more than 130 migrate there every year.

Several types of insects live in Sierra Leone, especially in the thick of the forests. They include mosquitoes, bees, ants, centipedes, millipedes, locusts, grasshoppers, butterflies, dragonflies, sandflies, and spiders.

Sierra Leone's rivers, lakes, and coastal waters abound with sea life. Among the common species found in the Atlantic Ocean are bonga (a type of herring), tuna, butterfish, skate, grey mullet, and tarpon. Shrimp, lobster, and other shellfish are also caught in these waters. Barracuda infest the estuaries, as do crocodiles.

The bongo is a common creature native to the mountain forest of central Africa. A member of the antelope family, the bongo thrives in dense, cool, humid forests. The bongo is a shy and swift animal. It has large ears and a short mane. Bongos travel in groups of up to about 20. They eat leaves and roots, and they sometimes rear up on their forelegs to reach higher branches to feed.

FREETOWN

By far the largest city in Sierra Leone, the capital city of Freetown is a busy Atlantic port located on the shore of a rugged peninsula. About 25 miles (40 km) long and about 10 miles (16 km) wide, the peninsula includes a large natural harbor bordered by mountains rising about 3,000 feet (90 m) above sea level. Large streams flow from these high peaks into the Atlantic Ocean. Most of the peninsula consists of mountains carpeted with trees. In order to protect the city from flooding that would occur without the natural barrier formed by these forests, the government declared them natural reserves that cannot be cut down. The city's highest site, Leicester Peak, offers spectacular views of the city, the sea, and the mountains.

Freed slaves from all over Africa, many of whom had lived in the United States, Great Britain, and Jamaica, first settled Freetown in the late 18th century. Local ethnic groups, including the Mende, mingled with these new arrivals and developed a new ethnic culture and language called Krio. Freetown's harbor, the third-largest natural harbor in the world, is the center of the city's economy and handles the majority of the country's imports and exports. Other local industries include fish packing, rice milling, petroleum refining, and diamond cutting.

In the mountains just east of the capital are Krio villages originally built by resettled American slaves in the early 1800s. Named after British cities such as Hamilton, Kent, and York, these communities were built in the style of British and American towns. They were also home to Sierra Leone's first churches, many of which still stand today. Saint Charles Parish Methodist Church in Regent is believed to be the oldest stone church with continuous worship in sub-Saharan Africa.

Also close to Freetown along the Cape Peninsula are many fishing villages, such as Waterloo, where Portuguese explorers first landed, and Tembo, which supplies Freetown with most of its fresh seafood.

People and traffic share a busy Freetown road.

THE COTTON TREE

Located in the center of Freetown is a large cotton tree that has come to signify the strength and perseverance of the country. No one knows how old the cotton tree is, but it existed in 1787, when the initial group of settlers from Britain, made up mostly of former slaves, established themselves on the peninsula. It was still flourishing in 1792, when a group of former slaves joined the settlement and gave it the name Freetown. Upon arrival, the settlers gathered under the cotton tree to pray.

The cotton tree grew up with Freetown. It has achieved distinction because of its grandiose beauty and central location, and it features prominently in most pictures and paintings of the capital city. Citizens still visit the tree to pray for peace and prosperity.

Freetown is home to West Africa's oldest institution of higher learning: Fourah Bay College. Originally called the Christian Institute, Fourah Bay College is now part of the University of Sierra Leone, which consists of educational establishments in different parts of the country. Among its branches are Njala University College, the College of Medicine and Allied Sciences, and the Institute of Public Administration and Management.

An estimated 3,000 men and women are currently enrolled at the University of Sierra Leone. The decade-long civil war disrupted the university's activities as it did all other aspects of life. The university lost infrastructure, equipment, and staff members. During this time, all departments relocated to the capital, Freetown. The government and the private sector are working together to rebuild the university.

OTHER URBAN AREAS

Most people in Sierra Leone live in or around Freetown. Nevertheless, the country has important cities in its other provinces.

BO Bo is the second-largest city in Sierra Leone and the regional headquarters of the Southern Province. With a population of about 60,000, the city is known as a center for diamond trading. It is also the administrative center of Sierra Leone. Several international charities operate from Bo, including the SOS Children's Village Bo. The city is also home to many volunteer workers.

KENEMA The capital of Sierra Leone's Eastern Province, Kenema is the center of the country's diamond-mining industry. Severely damaged during the war, Kenema is working to regain the charm it once had as a modern version of an American frontier town. Every storefront lining the dusty main street will restore its painting of large, cartoonlike diamonds with a sign advertising "Diamond Buying Office." Although diamonds now form Kenema's main industry, the village was originally developed as a trading center and a stopping point on the early railway.

MAKENI Before becoming the headquarters of the rebel forces during Sierra Leone's civil war, Makeni was a thriving market town, where tobacco was traded in large quantities. Largely destroyed during the war, the capital of the Northern Province—and the fourth-largest city in the country—is located approximately 75 miles (120 km) northeast of Freetown.

A street in Bo. The city's roads are being rehabilitated to improve transportation to and within Bo.

HISTORY

LOCATED IN A PRIME POSITION on the Atlantic Ocean in West Africa and endowed with plentiful natural resources, Sierra Leone has a rich, textured history. It remains home to at least 18 separate ethnic groups that have faced political, economic, and military challenges together. First a British colony and protectorate, the country achieved independence in 1961. The years since independence have been fraught with violence and struggle. Since 2002, however, the strong and united people of Sierra Leone have been working to rebuild their country and to provide a more secure future for their children.

ORIGINAL INHABITANTS

Little is known of Sierra Leone's history before the 15th century, when the first European explorers and traders arrived. Archaeologists have identified stone tools found in several locations as belonging to a Late Stone Age culture. The style of the workmanship indicates that these early inhabitants traveled north from the Sahara and sub-Saharan Africa, probably around the third century B.C. Later, another group of people, whose descendents today make up a minority of Sierra Leone's population, settled along the coast. They included the Sherbro, the Krim, and other related groups speaking the Niger-Congo language.

The majority of present-day Sierra Leoneans are descendents of groups that arrived in waves between the 12th and 17th centuries A.D. Most of these people entered northern Sierra Leone from an area called the Futa Jallon, which is located just north of the present-day Guinea-Sierra Leone border. In the 12th century the Limba and the Temne arrived from this region. In the 17th century the Mende migrated from the Futa Jallon as well. By the early 18th century the Futa Jallon had become a center

Opposite: **A *nomoli*, or carved human figure, from Sierra Leone dating back possibly to the 16th century.**

for Muslim religious activity, which often spread across the border into Sierra Leone.

Fighting over territory and resources was common, particularly as the slave trade increased. The Mende were known as particularly fierce warriors who conquered many neighboring groups to gain more territory and power. These groups soon began to share many cultural, religious, and social traditions. The Mende, the Temne, and other indigenous groups began to unite as more Europeans arrived, and after a new group of former slaves called the Krio founded a new city on the coast. Their future conflicts would include internal power struggles as well as tension with the Krio and the Europeans.

EUROPEANS ARRIVE

Probably the very first European to see Sierra Leone was the Phoenician Hanno, who journeyed along the western coast of Africa in the first half of the sixth century B.C. and wrote a colorful account of his adventures there. However, it was not until Pedro da Cintra, a Portuguese explorer, first saw the mountainous seacoast and named Sierra Leone in 1462 that the true history of the Europeans in West Africa began.

Other Portuguese traders soon arrived at the country's excellent harbor to trade in gold, ivory, and other goods. By 1495 they had built a fort on the coast to serve as a trading post. The Portuguese were joined by British merchants who made trade agreements with local chiefs. Throughout the 16th century, trade along the West African coast flourished, and it increasingly involved the buying and selling of slaves. Slaves were brought to the coast by African slave traders and sold to the seamen in slave markets. The seamen then sold the slaves to traders in the Americas and the West Indies.

THE SUPREME COURT AND *AMISTAD*

In an historic case that fostered the abolitionist movement in the United States, the U.S. Supreme Court issued the decision in *United States vs. the Amistad* in 1847. The case involved a shipment of slaves from Sierra Leone that had been seized by a U.S. Coast Guard ship, the *Washington*, while on its way back to Africa. The ship held 53 Africans who had been captured by two Spanish planters and put aboard the Cuban schooner for shipment to a Caribbean plantation where they would be sold as slaves.

On July 1, 1839, the Africans took control of the ship, killed two crew members, and put the rest out to sea. They ordered their Spanish captors to sail the ship back to Africa. On the way, a U.S. ship seized the *Amistad*, freed the Spanish, and arrested the Africans, charging them with murder. The court ruled that the case fell within the jurisdiction of the U.S. federal courts, and the case went to trial.

John Quincy Adams argued on behalf of the Africans to the Supreme Court. He defended the right of the accused to fight to regain their freedom. The Supreme Court decided in favor of the Africans, who were freed from custody and from the chains of slavery.

BRITISH RULE

After 1787, British abolitionists, under the leadership of Granville Sharp, settled 411 freed Africans at Freetown. In addition to ending the practice of slavery, the abolitionists' goals included promoting Christianity and Western civilization as well as increasing commerce throughout the region.

In 1808 the settlement of Freetown became a British crown colony. A new and distinctive culture, known as Creole or Krio, synthesized diverse African and European elements. Krio culture brought Christianity, the English language, and European goods to much of West Africa. By 1850 more than 50,000 former slaves from all over Africa had resettled in the colony. Cut off from their homes and traditions by the experience of slavery and repatriation, the Krio largely assimilated British lifestyles and language. They also built a flourishing trade on the West African coast. As time progressed, Sierra Leone's ethnic groups grew to resent the Krio's wealth and status within the expanding British presence in the country.

Encouraged by Krio activities, the colonial government extended its authority inland. In 1896 it established its protectorate over the

SIERRA LEONE.

An artist's impression of ships in the harbor off Sierra Leone around the middle of the 19th century.

hinterland regions of Sierra Leone, while the coastal region of Freetown remained a colony. At this time, Britain began to levy taxes and to place other responsibilities upon the Krio. Africans were rarely appointed to responsible positions in the expanded British administration. It was not until 1924 that colony residents were allowed to elect three members of the governing body, called the Legislative Council. Discontent over colonial rule mounted among the Krio and the indigenous groups, but the country lived in relative peace for much of the next 50 years.

THE WORLD WARS

As members of the British Commonwealth, soldiers from Sierra Leone served in both world wars. Soon after World War I was declared (1914), soldiers from Sierra Leone and other African countries under British rule were mobilized to defend their borders that adjoined German territories. They later took the lead in campaigns to remove the Germans from Africa.

During World War II (1939–45), Freetown served as an important allied base, and 17,000 Sierra Leoneans fought alongside the British.

Despite victories in each of these major conflicts, British economic resources and political power had been depleted. Shortly after World War II ended, a move toward granting independence to Sierra Leone and other British-governed lands began in earnest. The Krio and the indigenous groups supported the Sierra Leone National Congress and embraced a new political party called the Sierra Leone People's Party (SLPP). Founded in 1951, the SLPP negotiated the terms of independence with the British.

INDEPENDENCE

On April 27, 1961, Britain declared Sierra Leone an independent nation. Sir Milton Margai became prime minister. However, the SLPP found it difficult to establish support among the people, mainly because of its close ties to the chiefs. Opposition parties flourished.

When Milton Margai died in 1964, his brother, Albert Margai, succeeded him. Sir Albert attempted to establish a one-party political system but met with fierce resistance from a new political party, the All People's Congress (APC), led by Siaka Stevens. A member of the Limba group, Stevens was a trade unionist as well as a former SLPP minister who had served in the Margai administration.

The popularity of the APC and Stevens had its roots in the changing economic structure of the country. In the 1930s Sierra Leone's economy had been transformed from dependence on agricultural products to focus on minerals and mining. Much of the new mineral wealth was discovered in areas that had been quite poor and where the population had been disconnected from the political process. Shortly after Sierra Leone attained independence, Stevens emerged to unify the young people who felt powerless against both the Krio elite and the leadership of the traditional chiefdoms. Stevens and his followers in the APC soon became the dominant political force in the country. Stevens became known as Pa Shaka, the Father of the Nation.

MILITARY COUPS

In March 1967 a closely fought election gave a majority of the legislative seats to the APC and Stevens. The APC victory triggered several military coups. First, Brigadier David Lansana took over the government in favor of Albert Margai. Then, middle-ranking military officers who formed the National Reformation Council (NRC) took power. Finally, in 1968, army

President Siaka Stevens *(second row, seventh from right)* represented Sierra Leone at the Commonwealth Heads of Government Meeting in 1979.

privates and noncommissioned officers restored parliamentary government and Stevens resumed his position as prime minister.

In the 1968 legislative elections, members of the APC won all seats. Stevens then appointed an all-APC cabinet. Following the adoption of a new republican constitution in April 1971, the house appointed Stevens president of the republic. He was elected for a second five-year term in April 1977.

Stevens ruled Sierra Leone from 1968 to 1985. In many ways, his administration helped to unify the country and to stabilize political unrest. However, inflation and widespread government corruption led to growing opposition against Stevens's regime. Stevens and his ministers frequently used bribery and graft to retain their power. They also plundered the country's diamond and mineral reserves as a way of funding their government and lifestyles.

In 1970 the government was forced to declare a state of emergency after citizens staged riots in provincial capitals. In March 1971 and July 1974, Stevens claimed to have uncovered two attempts by the military to overthrow the government. The leaders of the plots were tried and executed publicly. In 1977 student demonstrations further disrupted the political scene. In 1978 the government enacted a one-party constitution that eliminated the country's multiparty democracy.

REVOLUTIONARY UNITED FRONT

It was during the politically chaotic 1970s that Foday Sankoh, a former journalist and photographer, became active in the country's political struggle. Sankoh left Sierra Leone and went to Libya, where he joined a guerrilla camp sponsored by Libyan dictator Muammar Qadhafi. At the camp, Sankoh met Charles Taylor, from Sierra Leone's southern neighbor,

Liberia. Together, the two men formed the Revolutionary United Front (RUF), a rebel group that would fight a brutal civil war in both Liberia and Sierra Leone. Sankoh frequently provided Taylor with Sierra Leone diamonds to help him maintain his troops, while Taylor provided Sankoh's troops with arms and training.

In the meantime, Stevens's APC party selected the army chief of staff, Major General Joseph Saidu Momoh, to succeed Stevens in 1985. Momoh appointed a civilian cabinet and attempted to distance himself from the corrupt politics of his predecessor.

CIVIL WAR

In 1990 President Momoh formed a commission to review the 1978 one-party constitution instituted by Stevens. His goals in doing so were to establish fundamental human rights and the rule of law and to strengthen and consolidate the democratic foundation and structure of the nation. His commission recommended the reestablishment of a multiparty system of government. The parliament approved a new constitution that embodied this recommendation. It became effective on October 1, 1991.

The ruthlessness of Stevens's regime had taken its toll, however. It was not long before unrest developed among the people of Sierra Leone again, this time fueled by Sankoh's RUF. Sankoh's troops swept through the eastern diamond-mining region, terrorizing civilians and causing widespread displacement.

Further reform was blocked by an April 1992 military coup led by Valentine Strasser, who dissolved Momoh's government, suspended the constitution, and halted political activity. Strasser then established the National Provisional Ruling Council (NPRC) to end the war with the RUF and restore multiparty democracy. The NPRC was later renamed the Supreme Council of State. In 1994, however, a negotiated cease-fire with the rebels failed and the guerrilla war continued. The death toll exceeded 20,000, and hundreds of thousands of Sierra Leoneans became refugees.

In January 1996, fellow officers ousted Strasser from office in another military coup. His deputy took over until the country's first multiparty elections in many years took place in February.

On March 29, 1996, the military government relinquished power to Ahmad Tejan Kabbah, the newly elected president. The new government achieved a cease-fire with the rebels a month later. In March 1997 Sankoh fled to Nigeria; he was put under house arrest and then imprisoned. Nevertheless he continued to lead the RUF and participate in negotiations with the Sierra Leonean government.

The multiparty democracy did not last; nor did the cease-fire. On May 25, 1997, rebel soldiers calling themselves the Armed Forces Revolutionary Council (AFRC) seized control of Sierra Leone's legislature. Johnny Paul Koroma led the junta (the group of people who lead after a military takeover) and ousted Kabbah, who fled to neighboring Guinea. Koroma and his supporters joined forces with the RUF. In the months that followed, the AFRC and the RUF devastated the country in a campaign of looting, arson, rape, maiming, and murder.

International diplomatic organizations, including the United Nations, universally condemned the actions of Koroma and the rebels. On June 2, 1997, a Nigeria-led West African peacekeeping force called ECOWAS (Economic Community of West African States) intervened. The peacekeeping force drove the junta from the capital and returned President Kabbah to office. Fighting between the forces loyal to Koroma and Kabbah continued, however. The AFRC and the RUF maintained control of the east and the north.

The war reached its peak in 1999, when the rebel groups stormed Freetown. At least 4,000 people were killed in the battle for control of the city. Widespread atrocities committed by the rebels continued in Freetown and throughout the eastern provinces. The RUF abducted children as young as 7 and 8, turning them into soldiers, workers, and sex slaves.

PEACE ACCORDS

On July 7, 1999, the two sides signed a power-sharing accord designed to set up a transitional government of national unity. This agreement called for the formation of an organization to investigate charges by human rights groups that the rebel forces had deliberately targeted civilians for death and torture during the war.

Under the terms of the peace accord, rebels convicted as war criminals were then granted amnesty, while many civilians abducted by rebel forces were released. The legislature also approved a bill that recognized the RUF as a legal political party. In October, the UN Security Council voted to send a 6,000-strong peacekeeping force into the country to monitor the cease-fire and to disarm soldiers on both sides.

Rebel forces numbering about 15,000 still controlled nearly half the country, which included most of Sierra Leone's valuable diamond mines. In 2000 rebels took several hundred UN peacekeepers hostage. Attacks on civilians escalated. Finally, in 2001, a peace agreement was signed by President Kabbah and the RUF, and disarmament and demobilization of troops and the release of abducted children resumed.

A man pours fuel over a pile of guns to set them on fire in a ceremony to mark the end of Sierra Leone's civil war in 2002.

A man and a woman in Kambia, Sierra Leone, rebuild a house destroyed during the civil war.

In what had become the largest and most expensive UN peacekeeping process in history, the final phase of disarmament in the diamond-rich eastern part of Sierra Leone took place in January 2002. In March that year, Foday Sankoh was charged with murder in connection with the killings of several demonstrators by his bodyguards two years earlier.

Presidential and legislative elections were held on May 14, 2002. There were nine candidates for president, including Kabbah (Sierra Leone People's Party), former military leader Koroma, Alimany Bangura (Revolutionary Front Party), and Ernest Koroma (All People's Congress). As expected, Kabbah was reelected, with more than 70 percent of the vote. The SLPP won 83 of the 124 legislative seats, while 27 seats went to the APC and two went to Koroma's party. The rebels did not win a single seat.

THE STRUGGLE FOR RECOVERY

Sierra Leone's bitter civil war claimed more than 50,000 lives, and thousands more people were wounded and maimed. The United Nations estimated that 400,000 Sierra Leonean refugees had fled to neighboring countries, another 450,000 had been internally displaced, and more than 200,000 women and girls had been subjected to sexual violence during the conflict. More than 300 towns and villages and 340,000 homes had been destroyed, and about 80 percent of health clinics needed rehabilitation or reconstruction. Fifty percent of teachers were absent from their posts. Eighty-five percent of livestock had been lost.

Today most of the displaced have returned to their homes to face the great challenge of rebuilding their lives and communities. In the meantime a special UN court in Sierra Leone is hard at work trying individuals for war crimes committed during the civil war. Koroma, Sankoh, and five other individuals were indicted in March 2003. The June indictment of Liberian president Charles Taylor, accused of supporting the rebels, sparked another political crisis in Liberia. Later that month, Koroma was killed in Liberia. Sankoh died of natural causes on July 29, 2003, while awaiting trial. War crimes trials continue today.

UN soldiers on Lumley Beach, Freetown, in a ceremony in December 2005 marking the imminent end of the United Nations Mission in Sierra Leone (UNAMSIL).

GOVERNMENT

SINCE ITS INDEPENDENCE, Sierra Leone has struggled to maintain an open and democratic society. However, its motto—Unity, Freedom, and Justice—remains a goal rather than a description. Although the country enjoyed a brief period of stability immediately following independence in 1961, governance of Sierra Leone has been chaotic at best since the death of its first prime minister, Sir Milton Margai, in 1967.

The country's latest constitution, enacted in 1991, sets forth a republic, which is a government led by elected officials, including a president and representatives, who in turn are responsible for governing the country according to the law. Today Sierra Leone supports a multiparty democracy. Its president and vice president were elected by a fair popular vote in 2002, following a bitter 10-year civil war.

Sierra Leone's constitution guarantees civil rights and religious freedom. Although the constitution also supports freedom of the press, recent actions against journalists call this support into question. Government corruption has been widespread. In 2004 Transparency International, a Berlin-based corruption watchdog organization, ranked Sierra Leone 118 out of 146 countries in terms of the amount of graft taking place throughout the government. In 2000 the parliament passed the Anti-Corruption Act and President Kabbah announced a "zero tolerance for corruption" policy in hopes of making the government more ethical and the country more attractive to foreign investors.

ELECTIONS

Like that of the United States, Sierra Leone's government has three branches: the executive, the legislative, and the judicial. Under Sierra Leone's current constitution, presidential and legislative elections are held

Opposite: **Sierra Leoneans gather at celebrations for the State Opening of Parliament.**

every five years. Everyone over the age of 18 is eligible to vote. The last elections were held in 2002.

Once elected to office by a popular majority vote, the president appoints a cabinet, called the Ministers of State, which is subject to approval by the parliament. In 2002 Ahmad Tejan Kabbah was elected to a second term as Sierra Leone's president. His party, the Sierra Leone People's Party (SLPP), also won a majority of the seats in parliament. Currently, 24 ministries assist the president and the vice president in running Sierra Leone. The president is also the country's commander-in-chief of the armed forces.

THE PRESIDENT

Ahmad Tejan Kabbah was born on February 16, 1932, in Pendembu, which is located in the Kailahun District in the Eastern Province of Sierra Leone. Although a devout Muslim, Kabbah was educated at Saint Edward's, the oldest Catholic secondary school in the country. He furthered his education at Cardiff College of Technology and Commerce and the University College Aberystwyth in Wales, United Kingdom, receiving a degree in economics in 1959. He later studied law and became a practicing lawyer in London in 1969.

Since returning to Sierra Leone in 1970, Kabbah has devoted his career to serving his country. In addition to holding government posts in all three provinces and the Western Area, he became a cabinet secretary in several ministries, including Social Welfare and Education. In the international arena, Kabbah served as deputy chief of the West Africa division of the United Nations Development Program (UNDP) and led the UNDP's work in several African nations, such as Lesotho, Tanzania, and Uganda.

Supporters of the SLPP point to a banner depicting the party's candidate, Ahmad Tejan Kabbah, during an election rally in Freetown in 2002.

Following Sierra Leone's military coup in 1992, Kabbah served as the chairman of the National Advisory Council, an organization designed to return the country to constitutional rule. In March 1996 Kabbah led the SLPP to victory in the country's first multiparty election in 23 years. His first objective was to end the civil war. He signed a peace agreement with the RUF just a few months after the election. The peace was brief, however, and a military coup exiled him to Guinea in May 1997.

Since his return to power in 1998 after troops from ECOWAS restored the peace, Kabbah has worked relentlessly to bring Sierra Leone back from its decade-long disaster. He was reelected to the presidency in 2002.

THE VICE PRESIDENT

The leading candidate for president in the upcoming 2007 election, Solomon Berewa has spent much of his life serving the public. According to his official biography, he was born in 1938 in the village of Yengema in the Bo District. He attended a Catholic primary school and then Christ the King College in Bo, from which he graduated in 1958. He also attended Fourah Bay College in Freetown and then traveled to England for further studies.

Berewa became a lawyer in London in 1973. As a lawyer, he first worked for the government and then formed his own private law firm in 1980. In 1996 President Kabbah appointed Berewa to his cabinet as attorney general and minister of justice. He led the peace talks between the government of Sierra Leone and the RUF in both 1996 and 1999. When President Kabbah was reelected in 2002, he chose Berewa as his vice president. Berewa has announced his intention to run for president in 2007.

THE JUDICIAL SYSTEM

Sierra Leone has a dual justice system consisting of Customary Law Courts and formal courts. Customary Law Courts are based on traditional customs, while formal courts are based on statutory and English common law.

The Customary Law Courts operate in all of Sierra Leone's 149 chiefdoms. A court chairman presides. No published laws exist, so the court chairman bases his decisions on customs and cultural practice. About 90 percent of all civil disputes, such as domestic matters and real-estate concerns, are handled by Customary Law Courts.

Recently, the Ministry of Justice announced a plan to investigate and improve the operation of the Customary Law Courts, which traditionally have barred the appearance of lawyers in the courtroom and failed to keep records of judgments and fines. The government hopes to institute standards and procedures for these local courts.

Above: **Vice president Berewa addresses the United Nations General Assembly in 2003.**

Opposite: **President Kabbah speaks during the Millennium Summit of the United Nations held in New York in September 2000.**

All criminal cases are heard by formal courts. This part of the system consists of magistrate courts that are supposed to operate in every district, as well as the Supreme Court, the Court of Appeal, and the High Court of Justice in Freetown. According to the constitution, all judges are appointed by the president on the advice of the Judicial and Legal Service Commission and with the approval of the parliament. Judges serve until they are 65 years of age.

The top judicial post in the nation is the attorney general, which is a cabinet post. Many of the justices, magistrates, and other lawyers are Sierra Leoneans trained in British universities or at Inns of Court in London. Judges serve until at least the age of 60 and must retire at 65.

The Special Court for Sierra Leone was established by the government and the United Nations to investigate war crimes.

SPECIAL COURT FOR SIERRA LEONE

Although the Sierra Leone Constitution of 1991 provides for freedom of the press, a Sierra Leonean law, Public Order Act of 1965, is currently undergoing scrutiny by legal scholars and citizens. The act criminalizes the publication, distribution, and even possession of material that may cause "public disaffection" against the president and other officials.

On October 5, 2005, Paul Kamara, the editor of one of Sierra Leone's most popular tabloids, *For di People*, was sentenced to four years in jail for publishing an article that questioned the integrity of President Kabbah while he was a senior civil servant in the 1960s.

Several international civil rights organizations spoke out in support of Kamara. Johann Fritz, president of the International Press Institute, said, "The truth is that Sierra Leone's press freedom is also in prison with Kamara and, until he is released, it is impossible for the country to claim that it has made a clean break from a period [during the civil war] when journalists were ruthlessly suppressed."

On November 29, 2005, the Sierra Leone Court of Appeal overturned the High Court's decision, and Kamara was freed.

Administration of the formal courts has been sorely lacking since the civil war ended in 2002. That year, only four formal courts operated in Sierra Leone. Since then, with help from international human rights organizations such as the UNDP, 19 formal courts have begun to hear cases.

LOCAL GOVERNMENT

The basic unit of local government is the chiefdom, which governs long-standing tribal communities. A paramount chief and council of elders, usually inherited positions, govern the chiefdom. Traditionally, the chiefdom governments have handled most local affairs. Before the British imposed their system of government on the people of Sierra Leone during the colonial period, chiefs acted independently to promote their communities' interests. Under British rule, however, most chiefs began to act almost as proxies for the British government.

Since independence in 1961, the governments of both major political parties have used the chiefs to consolidate and maintain power among the people. Certain larger cities, such as Freetown, Bo, Kenema, and Makeni, choose to have an elected mayor and a town council.

FOREIGN RELATIONS

Despite its difficult history and current instability, Sierra Leone has maintained cordial relations with European nations, particularly the United Kingdom. It also maintains diplomatic relations with the republics of the former Soviet Union, as well as with China, Libya, and Iran.

In addition to being a member of the United Nations, Sierra Leone belongs to the Commonwealth, the African Union (AU), the Economic Community of West African States (ECOWAS), the African Development Bank (AFDB), the Mano River Union (MRU), the Organization of the Islamic Conference (OIC), and the Non-Aligned Movement (NAM).

Designated Secretary General Kandeh Yumkella *(left)* of Sierra Leone and Secretary General Carlos Magarinos of Argentina talk at a United Nations Industrial Development Organization conference in Vienna in 2005.

U.S.-SIERRA LEONE RELATIONS

Sierra Leone has long maintained a cordial relationship with the United States. The first contact between the two countries occurred when American missionaries visited Sierra Leone during the 19th century.

In 1959 the United States opened a consulate in Freetown. In 1961, when Sierra Leone became independent, the consulate was elevated to embassy status.

In recent years, the United States has provided Sierra Leone with millions of dollars in economic aid. The United States continues to work with international relief organizations to help Sierra Leone recover from its devastating civil war.

THE NATIONAL PLEDGE

Like the people of the United States, Sierra Leoneans have a national pledge of allegiance created to help form a bond of unity among all citizens:

"I pledge my love and loyalty to my country Sierra Leone.
I vow to serve her faithfully at all times.
I promise to defend and honor her good name,
Always work for her unity, peace, freedom and prosperity,
And put her interest above all else,
So help me God."

As the country faces the next presidential and parliamentary elections in 2007, the hope is that all Sierra Leonean citizens fulfill that pledge and vote in large numbers and in peace to secure a fair, representative government and society.

ECONOMY

"NO LASTING ACHIEVEMENT is possible without a vision and no vision can become real without action and responsibility." So President Kabbah said when his country launched Vision 2025 in 2001, just after peace had been declared following the civil war. The purpose of the project is to establish short- and long-term development strategies to improve the lives of Sierra Leoneans by creating a strong economy and a peaceful democracy. The motto accompanying this project is "United People, Progressive Nation, Attractive Country."

During the civil war, Sierra Leone's economy suffered shortages, inflation, a flourishing black market, government corruption, and a deteriorating infrastructure. Seizures of foreign hostages, attacks on the mining industry by antigovernment rebels, and an influx of refugees from Liberia further undermined Sierra Leone's economy. By mid-1995, exports had virtually ceased, and roughly 75 percent of the budget was being spent on the war. By 1999 rebel forces had gained control of about two-thirds of the country, including the lucrative diamond mines, which they used to finance their war.

Since the end of the war, the government and citizens of Sierra Leone have been working together to find the best way to take the country forward. Poverty and unemployment remain rampant. According to the most recent official government statistics, collected from 1988 to 1989, Sierra Leone's unemployment rate stood at 25 percent, and nearly 80 percent of the people lived in poverty. Experts agree that the situation only worsened during the civil war. In 2002 the UNDP Human Development Project rated Sierra Leone the poorest country in the world for the second year in a row. Today it is the second-poorest nation, after Niger. More than 70 percent of Sierra Leone's population lives on less than one dollar a day, and more than 70 percent are illiterate.

Opposite: **A woman walks past a diamond dealership in Bo. Sierra Leone has substantial diamond reserves. Exports of the gem helped the country recover after the war.**

Nevertheless, Sierra Leone brings many assets to its new beginning. The country has abundant farmland to sustain its agricultural sector as well as plentiful mineral, water, oil, and energy resources. It has a vast natural harbor on the Atlantic Ocean that could play a role in improving Sierra Leone's status as a trading nation. Its beautiful beaches and rain forests could attract tourists, an increasingly important contributor to many developing economies.

Sierra Leone runs programs with the help of international organizations such as the United Nations and the International Monetary Fund, which continue to provide economic aid and technical support. Thanks to

Fishermen in Freetown repair their nets on the beach. Fishing is a major source of export income for Sierra Leone.

growth in the agricultural sector and diamond mining, with modest gains in construction and manufacturing, the country's gross domestic product (GDP) grew by a healthy 6.6 percent in 2004. Experts expect this to stay at around 6 to 7 percent through 2007.

AGRICULTURE

Because most people in Sierra Leone do not get enough to eat, many children and adults suffer from malnutrition. Today, as in the past, agriculture accounts for about 60 to 70 percent of total employment, but it generates a share of just 10 percent of the GDP. Crop production is mainly at subsistence level, and more than 60 percent of production does not reach the market. The critical food shortage has further impoverished already vulnerable groups, especially the rural poor, low-income urban families, and small-scale farmers.

In May 2002 President Kabbah made agriculture and food security one of the main goals for his second term. In his address to the House of Parliament on that occasion, he stated that a major thrust of his government's policy would be to ensure that "[n]o Sierra Leonean goes to bed hungry by the year 2007."

With most people having returned to their communities in peace, the country has a new opportunity to realize its huge agricultural potential. This will reverse its agriculture dependency and build food security for the people of Sierra Leone.

RICE

Rice remains an important staple of the Sierra Leonean diet, and most families engage in rice farming. About 64 percent of rice is produced in upland systems, while inland valley swamp land is the second-largest area devoted to rice cultivation. The main planting season is April through July. Harvesting takes place between September and January. The main challenge for rice growers is clearing the land of grass and trees, which leaves the countryside vulnerable to deforestation.

Because flooding is so common during the rainy season, many people choose to cultivate either a special type of tall-growing rice or a floating variety that can grow on the surface of the water. When the dry season comes in October, rice grains appear on the plants' stalks. Usually, the first of the rice crop is harvested in November. The rice heads are stored at a central site near each village.

Today the government funds a Rice Research Station (RRS) to conduct research on the best way for Sierra Leone to farm this important crop. It helps local farmers by conducting demonstrations of proper farming methods as well as providing seeds and other materials.

COFFEE AND COCOA

Coffee and cocoa are Sierra Leone's major agricultural exports. Since the end of the civil war, coffee's contribution to the GDP has risen from $0.2 million to $0.4 million. Cocoa's earnings have increased from $0.27 million to $2.59 million.

Coffee and cocoa are usually grown together. Most plantations are located in the forests near the towns of Kenema, Segbwema, and Kailahun in the Eastern Province. These areas were the hardest hit during the civil war, and most plantations suffered total or partial destruction. The government is working toward rehabilitating and expanding the cultivation of these crops, which once provided an important source of export income to the country's economy.

PALM AND PALM PRODUCTS

The oil palm is one of the most common trees in Sierra Leone, and this species provides several sources of nutrition for its people. Palm nuts are harvested by farmers to make oil and wine for local consumption and sale. Palm oil is used as cooking oil or solidified into butter.

For many years, farmers sold palm nut kernels to the government-owned Palm Kernel Oil Mill in Freetown. In 1994 the government attempted to make the mill private by selling it to a local company. However rebel forces vandalized the mill and shut it down after 1997. More recently a new company bought the mill and rehabilitated it.

Sierra Leonean women make palm oil soap to earn a living.

When fully operational, the mill will produce about 20 tons, or 5,500 gallons (20,800 l), of oil per day. Since Sierra Leoneans consume only about 20 tons of oil per month, the company hopes it will soon be able to start exporting the surplus. In addition, other non-edible products can be made from the excess, including laundry soap, toilet soap, cosmetic oils, and animal feed.

Sierra Leone has lagged behind other countries when it comes to oil-palm technology. However, the government, working with the private sector, is determined to move the oil-palm industry forward as a major crop for both local consumption and export.

MINING

Mining has always been vitally important to Sierra Leone's economy. In the late 1980s, the country earned about $98 million a year from mining. The onset of the civil war seriously disrupted this sector of the economy; since the end of the war in 2002, however, Sierra Leone has been working to fulfill the promise of its rich natural resources.

Although diamonds form the principal component of the country's mining sector, bauxite, hematite (an iron ore), and rutile also contribute to this growing industry. Traditionally mining has contributed about 20 percent of the nation's GDP.

DIAMONDS

The first diamond in Sierra Leone was discovered in 1930. The sparkling gem has represented the country's greatest potential as well as its bloodiest commodity. Sierra Leone's established diamond fields are located largely in the southeast and east of the country and cover more than one-quarter of its area. The fields are concentrated in the districts of Bo, Kono, and Kenema, and are mainly situated in the drainage areas of the Sewa, Bafi, Woa, Mano, and Moa rivers.

Sierra Leone is renowned for both the quality and the size of its diamonds. The third-largest diamond ever found—now called the Star of Sierra Leone—was mined in the territory in 1972. In the rough, the diamond weighs almost 0.5 pound or 968.8 carats. The rough stone was eventually cut into 17 exquisite individual diamonds, six of which are now set in the Star of Sierra Leone brooch.

Rebel forces in Sierra Leone and Liberia used diamonds mined in Sierra Leone to fund their wars. Because of the connection between violence and the diamond trade, the United Nations banned the importation or purchase of Sierra Leone diamonds that were not certified by the government.

Because of the turmoil and controversy over the country's diamond trade, diamonds fell from more than 80 percent to only a little more than 20 percent of the country's exports. However, in 2001, the United Nations, governments of diamond-producing countries, and diamond industry representatives came

together to create a diamond certification program known as the Kimberly Process. Sierra Leone was among the first 50 countries to accept and implement the process on January 1, 2003. According to a November 3, 2004, report in the *UN Chronicle*, legal exports from Sierra Leone rose from $1.3 to $25.9 million worth of diamonds during the following 12 months. Before the process, as much as 20 percent of rough-diamond output was considered to be unregulated and therefore available for money laundering or arms dealing. According to statistics collected by the World Bank, the total value of diamond exports in 2004 was approximately $100 million.

RUTILE AND OTHER MINERALS

Sierra Leone possesses one of the largest natural rutile reserves in the world. Manufacturers obtain titanium dioxide, which is used to produce aircraft and spacecraft, and titanium, used to make white paint, from this mineral. Rutile accounted for approximately one-half of Sierra Leone's export earnings before the civil war.

The mineral is found chiefly in the coastal zone of the Southern Province, although some deposits have been discovered in the north between the Great Scarcies and Little Scarcies rivers. It was first discovered in 1954 in the Lanti River in the Southern Province.

First discovered in northern Sierra Leone in 1920 and 1921, bauxite is another mineral important to the country's economy. It is from this ore that aluminum is manufactured. Bauxite mining in the Mokanji area of the Southern Province was begun by the Sierra Leone Ore and Metal Company in 1963. This mine alone produced about 735,000 tons of bauxite in 1994. Operations were overrun in 1995 during the civil war.

In addition to diamonds, rutile, and bauxite, Sierra Leone's land holds stores of gold, iron, and other minerals. In 2005 the rutile mines were reopened. Developing these important resources remains an important goal for the government. The government continues to seek private investment as well as economic aid from other countries and from international organizations to stimulate the mining industry.

TRANSPORTATION

Sierra Leone has a highway system, although all but about 620 miles (1,000 km) of it remains unpaved. A program developed and managed by the Sierra Leone Roads Authority (SLRA) plans to repave the West African roadway during the next several years.

About two hours away from Freetown, across the harbor, is the country's only international airport, Lungi Airport. A helicopter service is available to take arriving passengers to the Lumley Beach airport in Freetown, which is about a 20-minute trip. An hour-long ferry into Freetown is also available. The country has about 14 local airstrips, many of which were damaged during the war. Sierra Leone does not own a national airline for passengers, although Sierra National Airlines handles cargo. Efforts

Opposite: **A technician repairs a landline in Freetown. In the background is an advertisement for a major mobile telephone company in Sierra Leone.**

Below: **A ship in the harbor at Freetown. Although harbor facilities are in need of improvement, regular shipping services connect the city with American, British, Chinese, European, and Japanese ports.**

are now underway to modernize and expand Lungi Airport as well as the domestic airstrips. The government and private-sector investors are now planning to build a new international airport on Sherbro Island in hopes of attracting more tourists to the white sandy beaches and clear blue waters of Sierra Leone's Atlantic coast.

Serving as Sierra Leone's chief port, Freetown has one of the best natural harbors along the West African coast. The country exports most of its goods to Britain and the United States, while the bulk of its imports come from China, Britain, and Germany. There is little trade with other African states. While small boat owners handle most internal river transportation, the government is attempting to develop more efficient

and reliable methods of carrying goods from the interior to the Freetown port.

ENERGY

Energy and power are lacking throughout Sierra Leone. In the city of Freetown, electricity comes on only about once every few weeks. The electricity sector is led by the state-owned National Power Authority. Power shortages and outages are frequent.

Fortunately, Sierra Leone has great potential to generate hydropower, which is energy produced by the force of water. The Bumbuna Dam will eventually supply all of Sierra Leone with electricity. In 1975 construction began. The war put the project on hold for 12 years. Located on the upper reaches of the Seli River about 125 miles (200 km) northeast of Freetown, the dam is considered crucial to the development of post-war Sierra Leone. In 2003 the World Bank offered financial and technical assistance to the project. The dam is expected to provide enough energy to sustain Freetown and much of northern Sierra Leone by the end of 2006.

TELECOMMUNICATIONS

Sierra Leone's primary telecommunications provider is Sierra Leone Telecommunications

Limited (SIERRATEL). Telephone service remains sporadic, and not many people in Sierra Leone own telephones. For a population of about 6 million, there were only 24,000 land lines and 67,000 mobile telephones in the country as of 2002, the last year for which official records exist. On July 26, 1996, SIERRATEL launched Internet services. Internet usage is sure to grow rapidly as infrastructure improves.

DEVELOPING NEW OPPORTUNITIES

Sierra Leone is a member of the Economic Community of West African States (ECOWAS), which strengthens trading partnerships among Sierra Leone and its neighbors Gambia, Guinea, Ghana, and Nigeria. Sierra Leone also belongs to the West African Monetary Zone (WAMZ). WAMZ is responsible for pegging the currencies of ECOWAS members

A Sierra Leonean woman speaks on a mobile telephone while her companion listens to a small radio.

to the U.S. dollar. One potential result may be the establishment of a common currency among the ECOWAS countries, easing trade and encouraging international investment.

Sierra Leone's government also focuses on tourism as it attempts to solidify and expand the country's economy. Sierra Leone has some of the most beautiful beaches, mountain peaks, and rain forests in West Africa, and tourism in these areas has become one of the most dynamic sectors of the new economy. Currently, an estimated 4,000 Sierra Leoneans work in the tourist industry, mostly in the capital. Increased employment opportunities and revenue are among the goals of expanding tourism in Sierra Leone. Now that peace and stability have returned to the country, the National Tourist Board hopes that more and more people from around the world will visit.

A doorman at the Bintumani Hotel in Freetown. Destroyed during the civil war, the hotel was reopened in 2003 by its new Chinese owners.

ENVIRONMENT

RAPID POPULATION GROWTH over the past few decades, combined with the damage from the civil war, has put enormous pressure on Sierra Leone's environment and its ecosystems.

Most Sierra Leoneans depend on subsistence farming to sustain their way of life. This practice, along with an uncontrolled expansion of cattle grazing, has resulted in problems of deforestation and soil depletion. In addition, over-harvesting of timber has led to further deforestation as well as the loss of natural habitats for the country's wildlife. Finally diamond mining is a cause of soil erosion in areas that might otherwise be used for farming.

Although Sierra Leone faces many challenges—economic, social, medical, and political—as it recovers from the civil war, the government recognizes the importance of improving and protecting the environment. Without clean air, water, and other natural resources, the future of Sierra Leone would face further jeopardy.

The Ministry of Lands, Country Planning, and the Environment is the government agency in charge of the proper management of Sierra Leone's land, water, and air quality. The purpose of the ministry is to promote and achieve balance among several competing priorities, including urbanization, provision of affordable housing, and proper land and environmental management.

DEFORESTATION

According to statistics collected by the Food and Agriculture Organization of the United Nations (FAO) in 2005, about 38.5 percent of Sierra Leone's land area, which equates to 6,805,282 acres (2,754,000 ha), is covered with forest. However, deforestation of this land is taking place

Opposite: **River agriculture in Sierra Leone. The nation's economic needs influence the natural environment.**

at a rate of about 0.7 percent a year. The FAO estimates that the country lost about 24,000 acres (97,000 ha) between 2000 and 2005.

There are several causes of deforestation in Sierra Leone. First, most people in Sierra Leone continue to depend on subsistence agriculture for survival. Because of the turmoil of war, they have not been able to develop stable farming communities. Instead they cultivate one area for one or two seasons and then move on to another area. This practice of shifting cultivation is one reason for the loss of forest land.

The slash-and-burn technique of clearing land for farming has destroyed large forested areas in the heart of Sierra Leone.

Another reason for deforestation is the need for timber as fuel for cooking and to power small industries. Mining activities, particularly in the eastern and southern regions, and overgrazing by cattle are other causes. In addition annual bush fires destroy an average of 494,000 acres (200,000 ha) of woodlands every year.

Although most deforestation has occurred in the upland areas, the mangroves along the coast are also being exploited for fuel and for rice farming. The loss of these trees means that inland areas are at greater risk of damage from storms. It has also meant the destruction of the natural breeding grounds of fish and other wildlife in the region.

Sierra Leone has a National Committee for Mountain Conservation. The committee is a permanent body whose mandate is to promote sustainable mountain development at the national, regional, and chiefdom levels, with a particular focus on biodiversity conservation, tree planting, watershed management, and inland valley swamp development.

SOIL EROSION

Many of the same hazards to Sierra Leone's forests cause damage to its cultivable land. The method of farming practiced by many Sierra Leoneans, in which they cultivate one area for a few seasons then move on to another plot, tends to deplete the soil. Overgrazing by cattle also degrades the land.

Another prime cause of soil erosion, especially in the country's southeast, is diamond mining. Since the beginning of the civil war in 1992, independent diggers have carried out much of the diamond trade. The resulting constant clearing and digging of the land causes soil erosion. In addition the holes left behind become breeding grounds for mosquitoes and the diseases they carry, including malaria.

WETLANDS

Wetlands—lands covered by water that form a barrier between permanently flooded deep-water regions and well-drained uplands—are among the most productive habitats on earth. They provide shelter and nursery areas for commercially important animals like fish and shellfish, as well as wintering grounds for migrating birds. Coastal marshes are particularly valuable for preventing loss of life and property by protecting the land from extreme floods and storms.

In the swampy environments of the carboniferous era some 350 million years ago, Sierra Leone's wetlands produced and preserved much of the

A river bed and mangrove swamps on the Freetown Peninsula.

fossil fuels (oil and coal) that continue to fuel economic development today. In Sierra Leone, the wetlands created by the Sewa and Male river basins provide fertile ground for diamond, gold, and rutile mining. Because of the country's need to develop these resources, destruction of the wildlife that lives in them has occurred.

The Sierra Leone National Wetlands Committee was formed in 2001 to address problems facing the wetlands across the nation. Currently Sierra Leone has one site designated as a Wetland of International Importance. The Sierra Leone River Estuary near the Freetown Peninsula is home to at least eight bird species and striking groves of mangrove trees.

The rocky banks of the Little Scarcies River are part of the Outamba-Kilimi National Park, which protects the natural habitats of a variety of animals, including crocodiles, hippopotamuses, and more than 100 species of birds.

Farmers of the Mende tribe harvest rice.

THREATS TO WILDLIFE

In 1972 the government of Sierra Leone enacted the Wildlife Conservation Act. This law prohibits the hunting of certain endangered species, including the duiker antelope, the bongo (a forest antelope), a species of monkey, the manatee, the pygmy hippopotamus, and the water chevrotain, which resembles a small deer.

Nevertheless, as of 2004, four species of mammals in Sierra Leone were listed as endangered by the World Conservation Union. These species included the chimpanzee, the Diana monkey, the red colobus monkey, and the wild dog.

Wild dogs are found mostly in plains and open woodlands. They are social animals that live and hunt in small packs, feeding on animals as small as a rat and as large as a wildebeest. Once found throughout Africa, wild dogs have diminished greatly in number for a variety of reasons, such as the spread of infectious disease and the loss of their natural habitat. Because of their reputation as fierce hunters of livestock, many people have shot or poisoned them.

Animals that are vulnerable to becoming officially endangered in Sierra Leone include two species of duiker, the fruit bat, the African elephant, the pygmy hippopotamus, the spotted neck otter, and the West African manatee. The manatee generally inhabits coastal areas, lagoons, and brackish rivers (rivers with both salt water and fresh water). Hunting and accidental capture in fishing nets are the prime reasons for the rapid decline in manatee numbers in Sierra Leone in recent decades. Timber cultivation and the clearing of trees for rice farming have also degraded the manatees' natural habitat.

LOOKING TOWARD THE FUTURE

Sierra Leone is party to a number of international agreements devoted to protecting the environment, including Biodiversity, Climate Change, Endangered Species, and Law of the Sea. The country also signed the Kyoto Protocol. Several non-governmental organizations (NGOs) work in Sierra Leone, including Friends of the Earth and the Concerned Environmentalists Action Group (CEAG). CEAG was formed when local farmers reported that the fertility of the soil was dwindling at an alarming rate. The NGO has organized a public-awareness campaign about the dangers of deforestation and soil degradation.

A dwarf Congo crocodile on a log in a swamp in Sierra Leone.

SIERRA LEONEANS

SIERRA LEONE HAS BEEN INHABITED for thousands of years. The population of Sierra Leone is made up of about 18 ethnic groups with similar cultural features. The largest are the Mende in the north and the Temne in the south. Smaller groups include the Limba, Kono, Sherbro, Susu, and Loko. Most of the Krio, who are descendants of the liberated Africans who first settled Freetown in the 19th century, still live in and around the capital city.

Due to various socioeconomic and cultural reasons, as well as the displacement of entire communities during the civil war, some members of all groups can be found in nearly every chiefdom, district, or province. In addition to indigenous groups, Sierra Leone is home to thousands of Liberians who fled from civil war in their country in 1990.

Despite the large number of ethnic groups, Sierra Leone has a fairly homogenous culture. The two largest ethnic groups, the Temne and the Mende, have absorbed many of the less populous groups. For instance, Loko people have been heavily influenced by the Temne who live near them, while the Kissi and the Gola have assimilated many aspects of Mende culture into their own. Intermarriage among all the groups has been common throughout the history of the country.

THE MENDE

Today, more than 2 million Mende—about one-third of Sierra Leone's population—live primarily in the south and east of the country. There are also some Mende who live in Liberia. The Mende speak a language of the Mandingo subfamily of the Niger-Congo group. Traditionally subsistence farmers, the Mende grow rice, corn, yams, and other crops. Those who live in coastal areas also fish.

Opposite: **Sierra Leonean children enjoy time spent together.**

Traditionally the Mende people live in walled villages with houses grouped in family compounds with a central plaza and council house. Like other traditional groups, they formed larger political units known as chiefdoms that were led by paramount chiefs. The Mende have a rich culture that includes the traditional arts of mask carving, music, dance, and storytelling.

The Mende created a unique system of mathematics. To count, the Mende use a system called *pu* (poo). *Pu* relates to the process of using two hands to transfer rice from one container to another. Because two hands have 10 fingers, the Mende's number system has a base of 10. The Mende word for the number 20 means "whole person," signifying

A group of Mende dancers in Sierra Leone.

the fact that a whole person has 20 digits (10 fingers and 10 toes). The Mende number for 30 is 20-10.

Descent and inheritance among the Mende is patrilineal, through the father. However, Mende men stand in special relationship to their mothers' brothers, whose blessings are even more important than those of their own fathers.

THE TEMNE

The second-largest indigenous group in Sierra Leone is the Temne, who live mainly between the Little Scarcies and Sewa rivers in an inland area stretching eastward from the coast. They constitute the majority of the population of the districts of Port Loko, Kambia, the southern half of Bombali, and Tonkolili in the Northern Province.

Kamajor tribal hunters. The Kamajors are a Mende group.

The Temne belong to a West Atlantic group that probably migrated into Sierra Leone from present-day Guinea in about the 15th century. The Temne claim descent from about 25 different ancestors, and each Temne bears the clan name. The clan names include Bangura, Kamara, and Koroma. Each clan is associated with a symbol or totem, often an animal or bird, which the clan members are forbidden to kill or eat. The clan name is transmitted from father to child. A woman belongs to the clan of her father.

Like the Mende, the Temne are an agricultural society, growing rice, peanuts, cassava, millet, and other crops. Those who live close to the coast also fish. Traditionally the Temne lived in villages or groups of villages that consisted of circular mud-and-wattle houses. Political units were chiefdoms led by chiefs who also had roles in the British government during the colonial period.

OTHER GROUPS

Among the largest of the other ethnic groups living in Sierra Leone are the Limba, who live in a territory of about 1,900 square miles (3,060 square km) between the Little Scarcies and Rokel rivers in the north. Like their neighbors, they grow rice and other crops. They are also expert brewers of palm wine, which they make by tapping the oil palm for its sap and then allowing it to ferment. The Limba maintain that they have always lived around the Wara Wara Mountains in the northern interior. Like the Temne, the Limba have clans with similar names to the Temne, including Kamara and Kargbo. Clan membership is acquired through the father, and no one is allowed to marry someone of the same clan.

The Loko are primarily farmers who settled in the Bombali District. The Port Loko District is not the traditional home of the Loko, but instead received its name because of the large number of Loko slaves shipped through the port during the slave trade. In addition to cultivating rice and other crops, the Loko are considered experts in creating products out of material derived from palm trees, such as soap, wax, and basketry.

The Vai, who live mainly in the Pujehun District in the Southern Province, largely practice the Muslim faith. The Vai are closely related to their neighbors, the Kono, with whom they probably migrated to the region in the 16th and 17th centuries. The Krim mainly live along the Atlantic coasts in the Kambia, Bombali, and Port Loko districts. These groups have inhabited this region at least since the Portuguese, who referred to them as the Bulom, arrived in the 15th century.

Young women in a north-eastern village in Sierra Leone decorate their hair with bright red tree seeds.

THE KRIO

Making up only about 2 percent of Sierra Leone's population, the Krio (also known as Creoles) are descendants of Africans who were captured and enslaved by the British or Americans, then freed and returned to West Africa. The first groups of about 400 free former domestic servants from England were settled near present-day Freetown in 1787. In 1792 they were joined by another 1,000 freed slaves who had fought for the British during the American Revolution. Another 500 ex-slaves arrived from Jamaica and became known as Maroons.

In the years between 1807 and the 1870s, when the transatlantic slave trade ended, about 50,000 people were taken from illegal slave ships

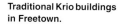

Traditional Krio buildings in Freetown.

and returned to Freetown to join the Krio already established there. The term "Krio" was first used in 1911, when the British took an official count of Sierra Leone's population. As opposed to most other groups in the country, such as the Temne and the Mende, the Krio were more likely to practice Christianity, to adopt English names, and to follow a European lifestyle. Krio families sent their children to Fourah Bay College, and many Krio served inland as missionaries, teachers, and administrative officers. Throughout much of the country's early history, the Krio lived on equal terms with the Europeans.

However, when the British made the interior of the country a protectorate in 1896 and more Europeans moved into the country, the Krio lost some of their dominance over medical, legal, and military jobs. Nevertheless, even as the number of Sierra Leoneans who identify themselves as Krio (about 10 percent of the population by 2005 estimates) has diminished, they still make up a large percentage of government and legal workers.

THE KRIO FULA

The Krio Fula inhabit the western peninsula of Sierra Leone near Freetown. Descended from two groups of Sierra Leoneans—the liberated African slaves who founded Freetown and the Fula people who arrived from the Futa Jallon region of present-day Guinea—the Krio Fula number less than 50,000. They are not of pure African origin, but rather, like other Fula people, are of Semitic descent. The Krio Fula are tall with lighter skin, straighter hair, and straighter noses than other African groups of Sierra Leone.

As is true for many peoples in West Africa, the Krio Fula subsist as cattle herders. Cattle—rather than money or even education—remain key to a family's position in society. The more cattle a family owns, the higher its status. The whole family participates in the endeavor: men are primarily responsible for herding the cattle, and women take care of milking the animals.

More than 90 percent of the Krio Fula are Muslim, although many also practice traditional animist religions. Their villages feature a central court that contains a mosque, the Muslim place of worship.

NON-AFRICANS

Sierra Leone has always had a non-African population of several thousand people primarily from Europe, the United States, and the Middle East. Since the civil war, however, many foreign nationals, many of whom worked for foreign corporations that were forced to close during the war, have left the country. The Lebanese have the strongest non-African presence in the country. They arrived in the country in the 1890s and soon figured among the country's most successful traders. The Lebanese in Sierra Leone are either Muslims or Christians.

THE SIERRA LEONE COMMUNITY

The people of Sierra Leone continue to struggle to recover from a civil war that killed more than 50,000 people, wounded and maimed hundreds of thousands more, and displaced at least 1 million citizens of the country.

The hope for Sierra Leone's future lies largely in the youth and vitality of its population: the median age of the people of Sierra Leone is 17 years, compared to about 36 in the United States. Hope also lies in the fact that the war was fought not over ethnic divisions but primarily over the bountiful resources that, if harnessed properly, can unify the country and provide for all its people.

WOMEN IN SIERRA LEONE

Although Sierra Leone's constitution guarantees equal rights for women, they still face both legal and social discrimination.

Women's rights and status under traditional law vary significantly depending on the ethnic group to which they belong. For instance, the Temne and Limba groups of the north afford greater rights to women when it comes to ownership of property and inheritance, while the Mende give preference to male heirs. On the other hand, women can become paramount chiefs—the highest local authority—in the Temne culture, while Mende society has no women at that level of government. The first wife in a polygamous Mende marriage often wields great power. She organizes the work performed by the family and is responsible for marketing any surplus crops.

In most cases, however, women in Sierra Leone do not have equal access to education, economic opportunities, health facilities, and social freedoms. In rural areas, women perform much of the subsistence farming and have little opportunity for formal education. The average educational level for women remains markedly below that of men.

LIFESTYLE

ACCORDING TO THE MOST RECENT government statistics, prepared in the mid-1980s, most Sierra Leoneans lived in small rural villages. In fact Sierra Leone had only four centers with populations of more than 20,000 and only one major city, Freetown, with about 500,000 residents. Today Freetown's population has more than tripled, largely because people have fled from war-torn areas in other parts of the country to the relatively safe capital.

Many towns and villages were damaged severely during the war. The government estimates that at least 350,000 dwellings were destroyed. Even today, the majority of homes throughout the country do not offer adequate sanitary facilities. Most people in rural areas live in houses built with mud walls and roofs of tin or thatch. Poor Freetown dwellers are no better off. Most refugees live in squatter settlements and inner-city slums. Rehabilitating villages and homes continues to be a priority for the Sierra Leone government.

DAILY VILLAGE LIFE

Until the massive displacement caused by the civil war, most of the rural population of Sierra Leone lived in relative isolation in small towns and villages. Those who have returned still depend on the food they grow on small plots of land near their homes or, if they live close to the sea, from the fish they catch themselves. Traditionally, men and women share the responsibility of gathering food, but women still do most of the cooking in outdoor kitchens. Men clear the plot for planting, tend to the crops, and complete the harvest.

The men of the village also build their homes from materials found in the area. Traditional villages consist of about 30 to 35 homes, which house about 100 people. Homes are organized around a village square that hosts weekly markets for the sale of common goods, such as food, clothing, and homemade items. Women may sell or trade handicrafts such as woven mats, spun cloth, and other items.

Daily life in the traditional African village begins at dawn with the children sweeping up the village and the women lighting the outdoor fires to cook the evening meal. Men harvest some vegetables or go to the market to gather food for the evening meal. Often the whole village eats together after a day spent in the fields.

THE ROLE OF THE FAMILY

In traditional Sierra Leonean societies, the basic social unit was—and remains—the household. The household consists of a man, his wives

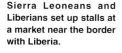

Sierra Leoneans and Liberians set up stalls at a market near the border with Liberia.

(polygamy is routinely practiced among all indigenous groups), his children, and often his brothers and unmarried sisters, forming an extended family.

In almost all cultural groups, descent and inheritance remain largely patrilineal—through the male members of the family. In traditional law, women were treated as minors and were not allowed to hold political office or other positions of status in the community. The man was also dominant in the household, and a woman was regarded as a dependent of her husband.

Traditionally parents or senior relatives arranged marriages. In modern Sierra Leone, however, most people choose to marry based on mutual attraction, religion, and other personal reasons. A practice that still occurs today is the payment of a "bride price." This is money or property given to the bride's family by the groom's family as way of making up for the family's loss of their daughter.

SECRET SOCIETIES

In most traditional West African societies, including the Mende and the Temne, children entering puberty become initiated into secret societies designed to prepare them to become responsible adults. Depending on the group, these societies also regulate sexual conduct, guide political and economic affairs, and operate social and medical services.

A nurse weighs a baby at the Princess Christina Maternity Hospital in Freetown.

Backed by the sacred character of their leadership and the spirits they represent, these societies stress the importance of preserving the group's culture and emphasize the rights and powers of the elders. Although young people become members of their own group's secret society, membership in similar societies forges bonds among young people of different ethnic groups.

Traditional secret societies are not universally beneficial to the community, however. In Sierra Leone and at least 28 other African nations, female circumcision (the removal of the external genitalia) is a key part of initiation rites. In traditional cultures, this practice is believed to prepare girls for marriage and motherhood. The United Nations Children's Fund (UNICEF) estimates that 90 percent of Sierra Leonean girls undergo this procedure as part of their initiation. The operation, usually performed by untrained villagers with crude equipment, often causes serious complications, including hemorrhaging and death, as well as complications in pregnancy and childbirth.

MODERN CHALLENGES

As rich in natural resources as Sierra Leone may be, the country—always among the poorest nations in the world—now ranks at the bottom of the list of underdeveloped countries. The lifestyle of its urban and rural citizens, therefore, depends on the need for better nutrition, more schools, and improved access to health care.

TAMING THE SCOURGE OF MALARIA

Sierra Leone's tropical climate makes the country particularly prone to infections of malaria. Various studies have shown that this mosquito-transmitted disease is one of the main health problems in the country and is the biggest single cause of death among children under 5. A 2003 study by the Sierra Leone Ministry of Health found that malaria caused 42 percent of child deaths occurring in the hospital. The same study showed that 11 percent of nursing mothers who died in the hospital also died of malaria.

Sierra Leoneans and other Africans have become resistant to traditional anti-malaria drugs, particularly chloroquine, and thus treatment often fails. A 2002–03 study found that resistance to chloroquine was highest in the capital, where it reached 60 percent, and in the rural east of the country, where 79 percent of malaria patients did not respond to the drug.

In 2004 the French-based medical relief agency Medecins San Frontieres (Doctors Without Borders) worked with the Sierra Leonean government to introduce a new cocktail of drugs, called ACT, that appears to be much more effective. Although ACT costs about 10 times more than traditional treatments, its life-saving benefits are priceless.

MEDICAL CARE Providing adequate health care to children and adults remains a top priority and an enduring challenge for the government of Sierra Leone. As of 2005, three years after the end of the civil war, average life expectancy in Sierra Leone is about 40 years of age—5 years younger than for people in other sub-Saharan countries and 30 years younger than for people who live in the United States. Access to clean water and proper sanitation is still scarce, leading to the spread of diseases such as dysentery and malaria. About 17 percent of all Sierra Leonean children die before they reach their first birthday, and 25 percent die before they reach the age of 5.

Another health problem facing Sierra Leoneans is infection with HIV and other sexually transmitted diseases (STDs). The spread of STDs increased dramatically during the civil war due to widespread rape and forced prostitution. As of 2001, about 7 percent of the adult population—or 170,000 individuals—were infected with HIV. Programs to educate people about the disease are sorely lacking. The government estimates that almost 50 percent of sexually active women of childbearing age are unaware of HIV and AIDS and thus cannot protect themselves from it.

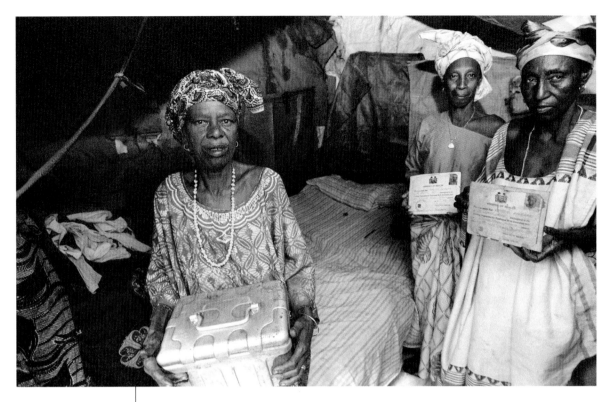

SPECIAL PROBLEMS FOR WOMEN A pregnant woman in Sierra Leone is more likely to die of childbirth complications than anywhere else in the world. Mothers die in 1,800 of every 100,000 live births, according to the UNICEF 2005 global report. One reason for this high rate of maternal mortality is that many pregnant Sierra Leonean women rely on traditional birth attendants instead of trained medical personnel. These attendants are usually women from the community who have received no formal education.

EDUCATION Throughout its history, Sierra Leone has had a strong educational base. At one point, the country was known as the Athens of West Africa because of its high level of education and training programs, particularly at Fourah Bay College and Njala University College, both now located in Freetown.

Three decades of poor governance and civil war, however, have greatly undermined Sierra Leone's educational system. Today only about

30 percent of the adult population can read or write and only about 40 percent of children attend school on a daily basis. Many school buildings have been destroyed. Most supplies were raided by rebel forces, and nearly all teachers were forced to flee.

Children were commonly used as soldiers in the civil war and as laborers in the diamond mines in the northeast of the country. Despite government efforts to get children back into schools, thousands of children still labor in the mines to help their impoverished families survive. Some child laborers are as young as 7, and most work as many as 10 or 12 hours a day. They perform hard labor, such as digging in soil and gravel and then sifting it with a pan for gemstones, instead of attending school.

The government's Vision 2025 introduced a new educational system, providing for students to spend six years in primary school, three years in junior secondary school (similar to junior high in the United States), and three years in senior secondary school. Finding qualified teachers and rebuilding schools remain integral to putting this plan into action. Nevertheless, according to the UNICEF 2005 Official Summary of State of the World's Children, only 50 percent of the country's primary schools are functioning today.

RELIGION

PEOPLE IN SIERRA LEONE are free to worship as they wish. Throughout the history of the country, the right to practice any religion has been respected by the government and by the citizens. On November 8, 2005, the U.S. Department of State released its seventh annual International Religious Freedom Report. The annual report found that "the government of Sierra Leone at all levels strives to protect [religious freedom] in full, and does not tolerate its abuse either by government or private actors."

Today about 60 percent of Sierra Leoneans are Muslim and 10 percent are Christian. The remaining 30 percent of the population practices traditional African religions. Many people combine traditional beliefs with those of Islam or Christianity, and interfaith marriage is common. Traditional African religions existed in Sierra Leone before Christianity and Islam were introduced. Many traditional Sierra Leonean religions share common points, including the belief that every natural object—from trees and stones to masks carved out of wood—possesses a spirit.

Historically, most Muslims lived in the north, most Christians in the south, and most people practicing traditional religions in the central part of the country. The civil war displaced hundreds of thousands of Sierra Leoneans, however, and it is likely that this pattern of settlement was disrupted.

Despite spiritual differences among Islam, Christianity, and traditional religions, Sierra Leone has always promoted religious tolerance and cooperation among its people. The Inter-Religious Council (IRC), made up of Muslim and Christian leaders, contributes to civil society and plays an active role in furthering peace within the country. The civil war brought Sierra Leone's religious groups even closer as they prayed together for peace and now work together to rebuild their country.

Opposite: **A group of children listen to their teacher during an Islamic studies class in Makeni.**

ISLAM

Islam came to Sierra Leone largely through peaceful means by traders, missionaries, and teachers. In the early 18th century, however, Islamic groups in the Futa Jallon in present-day Guinea invaded Sierra Leone and forced the conversion of people in northern Sierra Leone. Today people of many ethnic groups practice Islam. Muslims are now the largest and fastest-growing religious group in the country. Islam is popular among Sierra Leoneans for many reasons. First, it is one of West Africa's oldest religions. Further, it preaches equality and brotherhood, goals that appeal to Sierra Leoneans already known for their religious and ethnic tolerance.

Muslims in Bo, capital of the Southern Province.

The practice of Islam in Sierra Leone shares many traits with traditional religions. Prayers to Allah are brought to him from ancestor spirits just as they are in Sierra Leone's indigenous faiths. Words from the Islamic holy book, the Koran, are believed to have special power, much as natural objects do in traditional religions. Polygamy, the taking of more than one wife, is allowed in both traditional African religions and Islam.

Most African Muslims in Sierra Leone are Sunni, which is one of the two main divisions of Islam. The Lebanese Muslims who live in Sierra Leone are Shiites, the other division. All Muslims traditionally pray five times a day: at sunset, night, dawn, noon, and afternoon. Friday is the primary holiday. Other important times include the month-long fast of Ramadan. Strict Muslims do not belong to secret societies, but Muslims who are less conservative will mix traditional religion with Islam.

Opposite: **A member of the Temne tribe dons a traditional "sorcerer bird" mask and costume.**

TRADITIONAL RELIGIONS

All of the traditional religions in Sierra Leone believe in a single great being that created the world and provided the people with everything they needed to live. Each group has a different name for this being, but most portray him as masculine and benevolent. He is remote from people and does not judge them.

According to Mende tradition, Ngewo is the creator and ruler of the universe. Ancestors and other spirits, called *nga-fa*, assist Ngewo. All manifestations of the spirit, including the masks used in the performance of religious ceremonies, are considered *nga-fa*. On the other hand, the Temne call the supreme being Kru Masaba, while the Sherbro refer to him as Hobatoke.

Traditional groups also believe in spirits who are more involved in day-to-day life than the supreme being. The spirits of dead ancestors are particularly important. Believed to be able to help the living through direct action or by carrying prayers to the supreme being, ancestral spirits also are respected as the source and guardians of all knowledge. Another group of spirits is associated with natural phenomena such as rivers, rocks, and waterfalls. Sierra Leoneans believe that these things have human emotions and supernatural powers. Finally, there are spirits associated with the secret societies of traditional African groups. These spirits provide the power and enforce the rules of these societies.

To communicate with the spirit world, traditional Sierra Leoneans usually go through diviners and traditional healers, members of their groups whom they believe hold special powers. Diviners are believed to be able to look into the spirit world in order to locate the spirit responsible for an individual's or group's misfortune. They also may be able to see the future. Alone or with the help of a traditional healer, diviners also can diagnose illnesses and treat them with herbs. In return for the protection of the spirits and in order to appease offended spirits, followers perform certain rituals and ceremonies.

Belief in sorcery and witchcraft is also common among traditional African religions. Some witches are considered evil and others good, but all of them have special powers to harm or heal through the use of charms, omens, and curses.

THE IMPORTANCE OF MASKS

Masks are extremely important to the practice of traditional religions in Sierra Leone. People carve them in order to please the spirits. Those who wear the masks during ceremonies hope that they will be possessed by the spirits. Masks used in religious ceremonies are considered sacred and are used to hide the identity of the people wearing them. In many traditional cultures, the masks depict female faces but are worn by men. Wearing masks helps people feel that they are taking on the identity of what the mask suggests or represents. All but one mask are worn by men. The Bondo helmet mask, associated primarily with the Mende Sande Society, is the only known mask exclusively worn by women.

Young Sierra Leoneans take part in a religious service at a counselling center in Freetown.

CHRISTIANITY

Despite centuries of British colonial rule, only about 10 percent of Sierra Leone's population identifies itself as Christian. The Christian population is found mainly on the Freetown Peninsula. In contrast to many other African countries, Sierra Leone was not introduced to Christianity by white missionaries. Instead, the newly freed slaves who founded Freetown had been converted while captive in Europe or America, and they brought their new religion with them. For the most part, they were Methodists or Baptists. They began to build churches and chapels as soon as they arrived at Freetown. Some of these buildings still stand today.

The first white missionaries arrived in 1804. They belonged to the Church Missionary Society under the auspices of the Church of England. The Missionary Society founded Fourah Bay College, the oldest college in West Africa, in part to train Krio missionaries to bring Christianity inland. Later, American missionaries became active throughout the country as well. Roman Catholicism was introduced to Sierra Leone in 1859. Catholics founded several educational institutions, including two secondary schools, Saint Edward in Freetown and Christ the King in Bo.

Resistance to Christianity among the Sierra Leoneans exists because Christian tenets are very different from those of traditional religions. The practices of polygamy, ancestor worship, and membership in secret societies—all crucial to indigenous beliefs—are incompatible with Christian beliefs. Nevertheless, several leaders of the Sierra Leonean government have been Christian, including the first two prime ministers—Sir Milton Margai, who was a Methodist, and his brother Albert Margai, who was a Roman Catholic.

Saint George's Cathedral in Freetown.

LANGUAGE

SIERRA LEONE IS RICH in languages. Each of its approximately 18 indigenous ethnic groups speaks a slightly different language within the larger Niger-Congo group of languages. The official language used in schools and in government documents is English. Most people speak Krio, a mixture of African, English, and other languages. Therefore it is not unusual for a child in Sierra Leone to grow up learning four different languages: that of their parents' ethnic group, that of a neighboring group, Krio, and English. There are several immigrant groups, particularly the Lebanese, who speak their own language in addition to Krio and English.

TRADITIONAL LANGUAGES

Sierra Leone's two principal traditional languages are Mende and Temne, each spoken as a first language by about one-third of the population and as a second language by many more. The Mende language is one of the approximately 50 Mande languages, which are spoken by about 20 million people in several West African countries. This linguistic group is part of the Niger-Congo family.

Six original systems of writing have been developed for the Mande languages of West Africa. The first of these was devised by a Liberian named Momulu Bukele in 1830. The second was developed by a Sierra Leonean named Kisimi Kamara in 1921.

Kisimi claimed to have experienced a vision urging him to create a written form of his language. Born in an isolated rural village in the Pujehun District, Kisimi had no formal education. However, he recognized that the British, who ruled the country at that time, had gained much of their status because they could read and write. He wanted his people to enjoy the same privileges.

Over a period of several weeks, Kisimi developed what linguists call a syllabary, which is a set of characters each representing a sound or syllable. Kisimi's syllabary for the Mende language consisted of 195 characters. He named the system *Ki-ka-ku* for the first three letters of the syllabary. During the 1920s and 1930s, Kisimi taught the language in a village school he built himself. *Ki-ka-ku* became popular among the Mende for record-keeping and correspondence. The system fell into disuse during the 1940s, however, when the ruling British government began teaching Mende and other African languages using the Latin alphabet.

The written alphabet most widely used by Mande speakers was developed in 1949 by Souleymane Kante, a native of Guinea. He called

A vendor displays an array of books at a street stall in Freetown. Most books available in Sierra Leone are imported, but efforts are being made to raise the level of literacy and facilitate the growth of local literature.

his system the *N'Ko* alphabet. In most Mande languages, the pronoun *N* means "I" and the verb *ko* means "say." In Sierra Leone, the *N'ko* alphabet is used to write Mende and related Mande languages. It is written from right to left in horizontal lines. Diacritical marks placed below a vowel indicate a nasal sound, while diacritical marks placed above a vowel indicate the length or tone of the sound.

The Temne language is one of approximately 40 languages in the West Atlantic family. Like Mende, the West African linguistic group belongs to the Niger-Congo group. Its written language developed largely through the work of missionaries, both African and European, and uses the Latin alphabet. During the 1980s, the Sierra Leonean government made it mandatory for certain textbooks to be written in Temne and taught to all Temne-speaking students. An effort to expand this program has been renewed as the country continues its rebuilding process.

KRIO

No matter their ethnic background, most people in Sierra Leone speak Krio, a language that mixes traditional African languages with English. Created primarily by ex-slaves who came to Sierra Leone from Jamaica during the 18th century, Krio is the lingua franca—the hybrid language used in commerce and trade among people who speak different languages—of Sierra Leone.

Krio is also known as Creole. The term "creole" derives from the Portuguese word *crioulo*, meaning a person of European ancestry born and raised abroad. A creole language, known as Krio in Sierra Leone, is a natural language that arises from languages in contact with one another. Creole languages are related to pidgin languages. Pidgin is a simplification of a base language with generous contributions from other languages.

Like creole languages, pidgin is used to fulfill special, usually temporary, communication needs. Pidgins have been used by sailors, traders, and pirates. They are native to no one; in other words, no one speaks a pidgin as a first language. Since a pidgin is used only for certain kinds of communication, it is restricted in form and usage. However, when a pidgin becomes the native language of an individual (and many individuals who form a speech community), a creole language is born.

Although creole languages are often regarded negatively because of their relation to pidgins, a creole language is not just a simplified form of a given language. It is a full-fledged language that is capable of serving all the intellectual, psychological, and social needs of its speakers. In addition to Krio in Sierra Leone, there are many other creole languages in use around the world. They include Afrikaans, a Dutch-based creole language; Neo-Melanesian, an English-based creole language; Chamorro, often regarded as a Spanish-based creole language; and a number of French-based creole languages, such as the Creole used in Haiti.

KRIO WORDS AND PHRASES

In Sierra Leone, Krio is written phonetically in the Latin alphabet. The following are some everyday phrases:

Kushe	Hello
Ow di bodi?	How are you?
Di bodi fine.	I am fine.
Ar nor well.	I don't feel well.
Tenki	Thank you
Do ya	Please
Ow mus for dis?	How much does this cost?

OTHER LANGUAGES

According to the last statistics available in 1991, about 180,000 people in Sierra Leone speak Fula, which is similar to the name of the region in present-day Guinea. The language Fula Djallon is also known as Pulaar, and those who speak it refer to themselves as *halpulaar*, which literally means "speakers of Pulaar." Most Sierra Leoneans who speak Pulaar live in the northern part of the country near the Guinea border. Like all other African languages spoken in Sierra Leone, Fula is part of the larger Niger-Congo group. Fula is also one of the base languages for Krio Fula, spoken largely in Freetown and its environs. Krio Fula combines Fula Djallon with English as well as other African languages.

A sign welcomes visitors arriving at Lungi Airport in Freetown.

97

ARTS

SIERRA LEONE HAS A RICH traditional culture to which all of its ethnic and cultural groups have contributed. Its arts and sciences are of such importance to the government that a special section of the 1991 constitution is devoted to its preservation and promotion. The section states:

> The Government shall: promote Sierra Leonean culture such as music, art, dance, science, philosophy, education and traditional medicine which is compatible with national development; recognize traditional Sierra Leonean institutions compatible with national development; protect and enhance the cultures of Sierra Leone; and facilitate the provision of funds for the development of culture in Sierra Leone.

Sierra Leone's civil war destroyed much of its infrastructure and left little time for its citizens to practice or enjoy the music, dance, visual arts, and literature that are so important for the country's future vitality. Today the government and the people are working together to keep Sierra Leone's traditional arts alive.

MUSEUMS

There are two museums now open to the public in Sierra Leone. The Sierra Leone Railway Museum opened in 2005. It was established by Colonel Steve Davies, Deputy Commander of the International Military Advisory Training Team in Sierra Leone. Working with about 15 young unemployed Sierra Leoneans, Davies transformed a shed of locomotives, abandoned since the state railway ended in 1974, into the country's first railway museum. It includes a coach for the 1961 visit of Queen Elizabeth of England to Sierra Leone.

Davies told reporters that the project "has captured the imagination of both that generation of Sierra Leoneans who remember the old railway with great fondness and also the country's youth who by and large have never seen a train before."

The country's other museum is the newly refurbished Sierra Leone National Museum. Today the building houses traveling and permanent collections of local art and artifacts.

THE FINE ARTS AND CRAFTS

Sculpture has been a part of the Sierra Leone tradition for centuries. Stone and ivory sculptures date from the 15th century. Masks carved in wood in human and animal form figure heavily in ethnic celebrations.

The Sande mask, worn on the head of the chief dancer during the Mende initiation ceremony for young girls, is perhaps the best carved figure in Sierra Leonean art. It is a stylized black head of an African woman. Her hair is braided in an elaborate fashion, and she bears a graceful, dignified expression.

A carpenter carves a cross out of wood in a village in Sierra Leone's Southern Province.

Ivory figures are characteristic of the Sherbro, Bullom, and Temne peoples of the coastal and northern regions. Many traditional artists sculpt human figures out of soapstone, called *nomoli*, or wood, called *pomtan*. They are used for ancestor worship, fertility rites, and celebrations to ensure abundance of crops.

In addition to creating masks and figures, many Sierra Leoneans use local materials to make interesting everyday items, such as baskets, pottery, and mats. Dyed cotton cloths called *gara* are made using dyes obtained from indigo and the cola nut. Many *gara* feature repeating patterns, while others are more abstract. Although most modern *gara* are made with machine-woven cloth, women traditionally wove the cloth themselves. The town of Makeni in the Northern Province is famous for its *gara* cloth.

Efforts to bring Sierra Leone's dynamic arts and crafts to a wider audience continue. In 2001 the National Tourist Board of Sierra Leone opened an arts and crafts center on Lumley Beach. The center sells many locally made sculptures, crafts, and clothing to the public.

MODERN ART

Although primarily known for its traditional arts and crafts, Sierra Leone has produced some impressive modern artists as well. Olayinka Burney Nicol is a visual artist as well as a dancer. She has performed throughout the world, including in the United States, when she collaborated with Harry Belafonte and Sidney Poitier during the 1950s. Hassan Bangura's paintings of Freetown and village life have appeared in museums around the world.

Born in Sierra Leone in 1970, Abu Bakaar Mansaray is one of Sierra Leone's newest figures on the international art scene. He spent most of his young life as an artist in Freetown. Mansaray derived his sculpting

A girl learns to weave traditional cloth at a center in Freetown run by a nongovernmental organization.

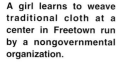

technique from a central African tradition of making decorative objects and toys out of wire and iron.

Mansaray took this art form to another level in the 1980s by inventing futuristic pieces that could produce light, sound, and motion. Inspired by science and technology, Mansaray also draws plans for pieces of futuristic equipment that are beautiful as well as inspiring to the imagination.

MUSIC AND DANCE

The most outstanding feature of Sierra Leone's cultural life, particularly among its traditional groups, is its music and dance. Every aspect of traditional social life—births, marriages, funerals, and initiation ceremonies—is marked by organized dancing, singing, and playing of musical instruments.

Typical instruments used for making traditional Sierra Leonean music include drums, a kind of xylophone called the *balangi*, and a type of piano called the *sansa* that is played with the thumb. The Fula Djallon, who live primarily in northern Sierra Leone, play a stringed instrument called the *kur*.

The Sierra Leone National Dance Troupe remains the country's most famous group of singers, dancers, and musicians. Coming from different ethnic groups, they perform stirring dances drawn from hundreds of years of tradition. In 1964 they won the international dance competition at the New York World's Fair, and they continue to thrill audiences in Sierra Leone and around the world today.

Male drummers are a traditional component of initiation ceremonies in Sierra Leone.

POPULAR MUSIC

Profoundly influenced by its rich traditional music and dance, Sierra Leone's popular music scene has been thriving since the early 20th century. So-called palm wine music, for instance, developed largely along Sierra Leone's coast and was a mixture of Atlantic sea shanties and African musical traditions. During the 1940s, calypso music from Barbados influenced the form.

The name "palm wine music" comes from its association with the drink of palm wine, which induces a mellow feeling. Also known as *maringa*, palm wine music features the guitar—first brought to Sierra

Children in Sierra Leone listen to the radio. Radio is recognized as a medium not only for entertainment but also for education. Programs are produced specifically for the youth of the nation and also offer them a platform to be heard.

Leone by the Portuguese—as the lead instrument. Often drums and the *sansa* accompany the guitar. *Maringa* is a very gentle music known for its intertwining guitar lines. Abdul Tee Jay is one of Sierra Leone's most famous *maringa* musicians. Although he now lives in London, Tee Jay's 2004 album, *Palm Wine A Go-Go*, is a tribute to his homeland.

As in the United States, gospel music has become very popular in Sierra Leone. Artists such as Vicki Fornah and Johnny Wisdom are among the country's gospel music stars. One of Sierra Leone's most important recording artists is James Bangura, known as Jimmy B. In 2000 he returned to Sierra Leone from South Africa and established a recording studio, Paradise Records. By doing so, he reenergized the Sierra Leonean music scene and encouraged new artists to emerge.

The United Nations Mission in Sierra Leone (UNAMSIL) radio station broadcasts music out of Freetown.

STORYTELLING AND LITERATURE

Until relatively recently, the African groups living in Sierra Leone had no written languages. Even today, only about 35 percent of Sierra Leoneans can read and write, and that figure is much lower among rural villagers. However, Sierra Leone has an extensive oral tradition that includes fables, legends, myths, and puns. Often older members of groups tell these stories to younger members in order to pass on traditional wisdom and morals.

The first book published by a Sierra Leonean was *West Africa Countries and Peoples* in 1868. It was written by James Africanus Horton, who also has the distinction of being the first African in history to graduate from a British university. Early in the 20th century, Gladys May Casely-Hayford wrote poetry and short stories, some of which appeared in British and American magazines in the 1930s and 1940s. Casely-Hayford wrote verse in Krio as well as in English.

Novelist and playwright Raymond Sarif Easmon first worked as a physician in Freetown before launching into a literary life in the 1960s. The theme of most of his works is corruption in government. His first play, *Dear Parent and Ogre* (1964), concerns bribery within the Sierra Leonean civil service. His other work includes a novel called *The Burnt-Out Marriage* (1967) and a collection of short stories, *The Feud and Other Stories* (1981).

Due to a lack of books in Sierra Leone, the Sierra Leone Library Board announced a new program called the Sierra Leonean Writers Series (SLWS) in 2001. The goal of the SLWS is to promote the publication of high-quality writing by Sierra Leoneans, writers of Sierra Leonean descent from around the word, authors who write about Sierra Leone, and to provide affordable reading materials.

LEISURE

ESPECIALLY SINCE THE END of the civil war, the government has encouraged peaceful and enjoyable activities to pursue. Due to lack of resources, such activities are few and far between in this poor country.

In 1965 the government established the National Sports Council in order to promote and develop sports throughout the country. Today the Ministry of Youth and Sports is responsible for promoting all sporting activities by funding staff and training athletes to compete at local, regional, and international levels.

THE SPECIAL NEEDS OF THE YOUTH

The youth of Sierra Leone suffered the most from the country's civil war. An estimated 700,000 of displaced citizens were children and youths. More than 9,000 youths were maimed, orphaned, or separated from their parents. Many were forced to become soldiers and suffered severe emotional and physical scars. Drug abuse and prostitution have become rampant among the youths of Sierra Leone, as have early pregnancy and HIV infection.

In 2003 the Sierra Leone government announced the National Youth Policy to focus on serving the needs of the country's youth, who, by some estimates, make up almost 50 percent of the population. The policy strives to achieve many goals, including helping young people to cope with the economic, social, and psychological effects of the war; providing health education; and mobilizing young people to replace the culture of violence with one of peace and understanding. The Ministry of Youth and Sports, along with a host of government, private-sector, and international partners, is working to create a better future for the children of Sierra Leone.

Opposite: **Shopping at the King Jimmy market in Freetown offers an avenue for social interaction.**

A group of boys play a game of badminton at a rehabilitation center for child soldiers.

GAMES CHILDREN PLAY

For decades, life has been difficult for the children of Sierra Leone. Still, they play together in innocence and in fun, especially now that a more secure peace has arrived. They play tag, chase and throw Frisbees, and—if they can get a hold of one—ride skateboards. Visitors to the country often remark on the friendliness and ingenuity of Sierra Leonean children. Government, private, and international aid agencies are now working to offer young people more opportunities to simply play with one another and to forget the challenges they and their families face.

One popular board game played throughout Africa is called Oware in Sierra Leone and Ghana. This game involves rows of holes, or cups, in which rest game pieces, usually pebbles or beads, that the players move. The board consists of two rows of six cups each. Each player has one row. There are two extra cups, not part of the board, for holding captured pieces. There are 48 pieces. At the start of the game, the 48 pieces are placed four to a cup in each of the 12 cups.

To make a move, a player picks up all of the pieces in his row and, moving counterclockwise, deposits the pieces, one at a time, in each cup he passes without stopping until all the pieces are used up. The players alternate taking turns.

A capture occurs when the last piece of one player's move is placed in a cup on the opponent's side and the number of pieces after the drop is either two or three. If the cup before that last cup also has two or three pieces, the player takes those pieces, too, and so on. The game ends when a player has no more pieces in his or her cups.

There are several versions of Oware. Some are called different names and involve slightly different rules. Commercially manufactured boards

Children play on a swing in the village of Hastings, near Freetown.

and pieces exist—and one can even download a version of Oware from the Internet—but most children in Sierra Leone make their own version using slats of wood or even holes dug into the earth.

SPORTS

Football, or soccer as the sport is known in the United States, is the national pastime in Sierra Leone, as it is in most of Africa and Europe. The Leone Stars, the Sierra Leone national soccer team, has continued to improve its standing within the regional league in which it competes. In

Three young men try to gain possession of a ball during a beach soccer match.

2004 the Leone Stars won the Four Nations' Peace Tournament involving Guinea, Liberia, and Gambia.

Indeed, 2004 was a successful year for Sierra Leone athletics in general. The national cricket team won the 17th West African Cricket Championship, and Sierra Leone athletes won eight gold and five silver medals in the West African Zone Two Solidarity Athletics Championship, which took place in the Gambia. Boxing is another popular sport, and thousands of people listen to radio broadcasts of matches whenever possible. Other common sports include basketball, tennis, and track and field.

In 2003 Vice President Solomon Berewa opened the newly renovated Wusum Sports Stadium in Makeni. Complete with a tennis court, basketball field, and soccer field, this sports arena is located in eastern Sierra Leone. It is sure to attract lots of spectators and athletes alike.

MEDIA AND ENTERTAINMENT

Sierra Leone has 12 weekly newspapers, most of which are published in English. *West Africa* magazine is usually available in Freetown. The state television, SLTV, broadcasts local football games, imported documentaries, news, movies, and television shows imported from the United States and Europe. Apart from the Sierra Leone Broadcasting System, there are several radio stations that offer a mixture of news programs and music. In 2000 a nongovernmental agency, the Center for Media, Education, and Technology (C-MET), was established to build Sierra Leone's media capacity through training and education.

Sierra Leone does not yet have its own film industry. Only imported movies are available on the cinema screens found mainly in the capital. As the people begin to rebuild the country's infrastructure and resources to expand entertainment and arts institutions increase, Sierra Leone is

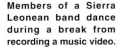

Members of a Sierra Leonean band dance during a break from recording a music video.

sure to begin to tap into the creativity and energy of its citizens to create a television and film industry.

As larger cities like Freetown, Bo, Kenema, and other district capitals continue to recover from the ravages of war, it is likely that there will be more entertainment arenas—movie theaters, restaurants, nightclubs, and museums. Efforts are being made to improve hotels and other attractions along the country's beautiful coastline. This will both expand tourism and provide an escape to locals eager to enjoy the sun and surf.

Today, tourists and locals alike flock to Freetown to eat in restaurants, dance in clubs, and gamble at the two operating casinos in the city. There are also markets that sell food and arts and crafts. The Government Wharf Market, which sells everything from general household goods to handmade crafts, is open daily. The King Jimmy Market sells fresh fruit, vegetables, and fish once or twice a week.

Sierra Leoneans enjoy the sun, sand, and sea at Lumley Beach.

FESTIVALS

SIERRA LEONE CELEBRATES several public holidays every year. Many commemorate religious occasions, while others mark important dates in the country's history. In traditional Sierra Leonean societies, the most important social occasions are those that recognize age-related milestones. Sierra Leoneans look forward to holidays as an opportunity to celebrate and to forget the challenges they and their country face.

By far, the most important holidays celebrated in Sierra Leone are two of the most sacred within the two leading religions: Christmas for the Christians and Eid-ul-Fitr (the end of Ramadan) for the Muslims. Those who practice traditional faiths mark important rites of passage, such as weddings and funerals, with specific rituals. However, since their first contact with Europeans in the 15th century, many traditional customs have changed to include Western symbols and practices.

On April 27, Sierra Leoneans celebrate the day they won their independence from Great Britain in 1961.

Opposite: **A painted and costumed dancer at a Soko secret society initiation.**

PUBLIC HOLIDAYS

New Year's Day	January 1
Independence Day	April 27
Christmas Day	December 25
Boxing Day	December 26

Moveable Christian holidays: Good Friday and Easter Monday

Moveable Muslim holidays: Eid ul-Fitr (end of Ramadan); Moulid ul-Nabi (birth of Muhammad); and Eid ul-Adha (Pilgrimage)

CHRISTIAN HOLIDAYS

As is true for much of the Christian world, Sierra Leone considers Christmas and Easter its most sacred Christian holidays. They celebrate Christmas, which marks the birth of Christ the Savior in the Christian tradition, just as people do in the United States. They decorate trees, gather as extended families to sing and dance, and exchange gifts. They congregate in churches to sing hymns, hear sermons, and pray. Many people who worship within traditional religions also celebrate Christmas, though more as a secular holiday than to mark the birth of Christ.

Holiday feasts also figure into the Christmas celebration. One of the most popular Christmas dishes in Sierra Leone is jollof rice, made with meat, chicken, tomatoes, onions, and spices.

A tradition carried over from the Mende and Temne cultures is devil dancing. While these dances occur on other holidays, Christmas is a special time for this fun-filled event. Much like the tradition of singing Christmas carols in the United States, groups of schoolchildren dressed as devils march through town and stop at various points to present brief 12- to 15-minute performances highlighted with devil dances and singing.

According to a November 28, 2005, report in one of the region's online newspapers, *Cocorioko*, the government-owned National Power Authority plans to keep electricity flowing in Freetown throughout the Christmas and New Year's season. Although the more common power outages may return thereafter, extra power at this time means that Christmas tree lights and other decorations will have a chance to sparkle. New Year's Day is also celebrated in Sierra Leone. Traditional communities often slaughter a goat to serve at large family gatherings to ring in the New Year.

Public holidays on Good Friday and Easter Monday make for a long Easter weekend for Sierra Leoneans. Christians attend church services and celebrate with family. An annual event taking place every Easter in eastern Sierra Leone, the Bo Peace Carnival, offers families a variety of activities aimed at promoting community building and sustainable peace. Musicians and dancers also perform.

MUSLIM HOLIDAYS

The three major Muslim holidays celebrated in Sierra Leone—and throughout the Muslim world—are Eid ul-Fitr, Eid ul-Adha, and Moulid al-Nabi. Eid ul-Fitr, the end of Ramadan, comes after a month of fasting. *Eid ul-Fitr* means "Feast of Fast-Breaking." It is often celebrated over three days, with the first day marking the end of Ramadan. After the special religious service, the focus turns to gift-giving with children. A ritual special among Muslims in Sierra Leone is the making and carrying of giant lanterns in a great parade on Eid ul-Fitr.

According to Muslim tradition, Eid ul-Adha celebrates the sacrifice that Abraham was willing to make of his own son Ishmael when he was commanded to show his commitment to Allah. At Allah's direction, the angel Gabriel substituted a lamb for Ishmael after Allah was convinced that Abraham would indeed sacrifice Ishmael to prove his faith. The name of

Opposite: **An African artistic portrayal of the crucified Christ.**

119

the holiday, *Eid ul-Adha*, means "The Feast of the Sacrifice." Part of the observance for many Muslims is the sacrifice of an animal in much the same way that Abraham sacrificed a lamb. Traditionally, Muslim families donate one-third of the meat to the poor, and the rest goes to their own holiday feasts. Children receive gifts to commemorate the holiday, and special prayers are offered throughout the day. Eid ul-Adha takes place on the 10th and last day of the hajj, the celebration of holy pilgrimage to Mecca, in the 12th month of the Islamic lunar calendar.

Moulid Al-Nabi is another important Muslim holiday in Sierra Leone. It commemorates the birth of the prophet Muhammad, who entered the

Opposite: **A Muslim man in Sierra Leone kneels in prayer facing Mecca.**

Below: **A mosque in Sierra Leone. Mosques are the center of Islam's sacred celebrations.**

world in 570. It is celebrated on the 12th day of Rabi al-Awwal, the fifth month of the Islamic calendar. In 2005 this holiday fell on April 21. On Moulid Al-Nabi, Muslims focus on the life and teachings of Muhammad by saying special prayers. A special part of this remembrance is how he forgave even his most bitter enemies, an important message for Sierra Leoneans as they struggle to move forward in peace.

PEACE FESTIVALS

The top priority of the Sierra Leone government and people is to find and sustain a peaceful democracy. To that end, many international human rights and aid organizations work within Sierra Leone to bring people together. For instance, Search for Common Ground, an independent, non-profit organization, is working to bring young boys and girls together to pursue peaceful and legal activities in their formerly war-torn communities.

The highlights of these activities are peace festivals held in provincial capitals every year. Youth groups work side by side, often with former rival groups, to host these dance- and music-filled events. The revenues earned at the festivals are used to fund community improvement projects.

In 2001 the UN General Assembly declared every September 21 to be the International Day of Peace, in

which, it is hoped, a global cease-fire and a day of non-violence will take place. The main purpose of the UN declaration is to "inspire humanity to reflect on, and commit itself to the mitigation of, the horrendous violence that makes life unbearable for people in every continent of the world."

NATIONAL HOLIDAYS

Sierra Leone celebrates its independence from Great Britain every year on April 27. In major towns and the capital, the event is marked with speeches by public officials and parades.

Body paint and elaborate costumes are essential parts of celebrations in Sierra Leone.

On the occasion of the country's 44th anniversary of its independence in 2005, President Kabbah addressed the nation. He spoke of the great challenges Sierra Leoneans face and the goals that the government has set to help meet them. He ended his address with a call for unity and an optimistic look at the character and strength of Sierra Leoneans.

"As a nation, our strength and character can be molded," President Kabbah said, "by our being united for the common good. History tells us that the United States of America, the most powerful nation today, derives its strength and power from the unity among its various peoples and races for the common good. There is no reason why we as a people cannot use our creative energies to develop this 'land that we love, our Sierra Leone.' Our predecessors did this before us. We too can do the same today."

WHITE BANDS AGAINST POVERTY

As part of the Global Call to Action against Poverty (GCAP), the world's largest anti-poverty movement, Sierra Leone joined other countries as they marked July 1, 2005, as the first international White Band Day. Sierra Leone's famous cotton tree in Freetown was wrapped in an oversized white band.

The goal of the event was to call upon world leaders to move forward on helping less-developed countries by instituting more fair-trade policies and canceling outstanding debt obligations. In addition to wrapping the cotton tree, Sierra Leoneans held a concert in the center of the city with local artists performing live music.

Sierra Leone was not the only country to take part in this effort. White cotton was wrapped around Australia's Sydney Harbor Bridge, Rome's Trevi Fountain, a huge mosque in Indonesia, Saint Paul's Cathedral in London, and Berlin's Brandenburg Gate.

FOOD

LIKE THE CUISINES of other West African countries, Sierra Leone's diet concentrates heavily on the fruit, vegetables, oils, and grains—including yams, plantains, cassava (a root vegetable prepared much like a potato), and groundnuts (peanuts)—that are grown on farms located throughout the country.

A typical West African meal is cooked with lots of oil and uses rice as a base. Peppers and chilies make most dishes quite spicy. Before the Europeans arrived, West African people, including Sierra Leoneans, traded with the Arab world, and thus Eastern spices such as cinnamon, cloves, and mint are often used in their cuisines. Despite centuries of exposure to European and American cooking methods, Sierra Leone's cuisine remains deeply entrenched in local customs and traditions.

More than 75 percent of the land in Sierra Leone is arable, or suitable for farming. Nevertheless, hunger and food insecurity remain problems. During the civil war, the agricultural sector of the economy fell to an all-time low, as did successful subsistence farming for individual Sierra Leonean families. According to a report prepared for the 2004 Regional Conference on Agricultural and Food Situation in Sahel and West Africa, Sierra Leone's domestic food production during the war was insufficient to support even 15 percent of the population. Since the war's end in 2002, however, some progress has been made.

BREAKFAST, LUNCH, AND DINNER

Like in the United States, people in Sierra Leone eat three meals a day: breakfast, lunch (traditionally the most substantial), and dinner. A popular breakfast dish is a stew called *yebe*, which is made of potato, cassava, or mangoes mixed with a thick broth. *Pap*, a sweet rice broth, is another popular breakfast food, which people often eat with sweet bread.

Opposite: **People trade at a food market in Freetown.**

FOOD

For lunch, Freetown has a good selection of restaurants that serve mainly European cuisine. There are also a number of cafés that serve variations of rice and palm oil-based meals. From vendors on the street, Sierra Leoneans enjoy fried dough, roast meat, egg sandwiches, boiled cassava, and sandwiches. A popular snack, known as *rosbif* in Krio, is a steak sandwich made of slivers of beef topped with palm oil.

The most common meal at night is *plasas*, which is made with finely shredded sweet potato or cassava leaves cooked in palm oil with dried fish and hot pepper. There are many varieties of *plasas*, including some made with beef instead of fish or with meat and fish combined. Many dishes are made with peanuts. Flaked and dried fish is often fried in oil and cooked with chicken, yam, onions, various spices, and water to prepare a highly flavored stew.

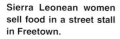

Sierra Leonean women sell food in a street stall in Freetown.

126

BEVERAGES

Most traditional Sierra Leoneans do not drink with their meals, but instead prefer to drink a glass of water before or after their meals. However, soft drinks such as Coca Cola and Fanta are locally produced, and others are imported from Europe or the United States. Sierra Leone Breweries Limited produces the popular *Star* brand of beer brewed from rice.

The most popular and common alcoholic beverage is palm wine. Tapped from the oil palm, the sap ferments to become a sweet wine popular in Sierra Leone and throughout West Africa. Making and selling palm wine is an important source of income to several groups in Sierra Leone, particularly the Limba, who have the reputation for making the best palm wine in the country. Imported wine made from grapes is available at restaurants and supermarkets, but it can be expensive.

A shop advertises coffee in Kenema.

127

Another prevalent drink is *omole*, a locally produced gin. Omole is produced using corn, sugar, water, and yeast mixed together in large vats and allowed to ferment for almost a month. Inexpensive to make, it is sold in markets throughout the country.

One of Sierra Leone's prime exports is coffee. Two indigenous coffee species are found in the rain forests that form part of the country's border with Liberia. However, drinking coffee is not particularly popular among most Sierra Leoneans.

COOKING AND EATING SIERRA LEONE-STYLE

Although many people in Sierra Leone have been influenced by Western culture, some choose to retain traditional cuisine and customs when it comes to food. Typically, it is the women and girls in the family who do the cooking, usually using a three-legged iron pot. Electricity and gas power remain scarce commodities, especially in rural villages, so charcoal or firewood is used to cook or heat food.

Women make a traditional porridge in a rural home in Kenema.

In traditional communities, males and females eat separately. In the male-dominated traditional societies, the oldest male receives the best food, such as the largest piece of meat or fish, followed by the youngest males. The women and girls eat what the men leave behind.

In a typical home in Sierra Leone, one large bowl of food is put in the center of the table and everyone eats from the portion of the dish right in front of him or her, always using the right hand. It is considered very bad manners to reach across to the other side of the bowl or to use the left hand. Also, talking during a meal shows a lack of respect for the food.

TYPICAL FOODS

Rice is the staple food of Sierra Leone. A common Sierra Leonean expression is "If I haven't had my rice, I haven't eaten today." Although Western utensils are routinely used in more modern regions, particularly in Freetown, Sierra Leoneans traditionally eat rice using their hands. They squeeze or roll it into a ball, dip it into a sauce or stew, and pop it into their mouths. The most popular soups and stews are made with greens, particularly the leaves of the cassava and the potato. Other common ingredients include palm oil, tomatoes, onions, yams, and red peppers. Peanuts, beef, chicken, and pork are the main sources of protein. Along the coast, fish and shellfish are also popular.

Women sell fresh green vegetables at a market in Bo.

GROUNDNUT STEW

1 pound stew beef
2 large tomatoes, diced
½ cup olive oil
½ cup crunchy peanut butter (groundnut paste)
1 large onion, chopped
1 large red pepper, chopped
½ teaspoon ground cayenne pepper
½ teaspoon ground cumin
½ teaspoon ground turmeric

Season beef with cayenne pepper, cumin, and turmeric. Let marinate for 3 hours. Brown meat in oil. Add some water and let simmer until tender. Remove from pan and set aside. In the same oil, sauté pepper and onion. Add tomatoes and stir briskly. Mix peanut butter with water to form a thin paste and add to vegetables. Add beef, stir, and allow to cook for 15 minutes. Serve with rice or boiled sweet potatoes.

FRIED PLANTAINS

Also known as cooking banana, plantains are members of the banana family. They are a staple of West African cuisine and grow throughout the area. Fried plantains make tasty treats, which are often served with a sprinkle of hot sauce on top or, for a sweet treat, a coating of powdered sugar and cinnamon.

2 to 3 plantains, peeled and sliced into ¼-inch rounds
1 cup peanut, soybean, or safflower oil
Salt, powdered sugar, or hot sauce to taste

Heat the oil in a heavy saucepan to 350°F (177°C) (use a cooking thermometer). Fry slices of plantains a few at a time until they are golden in color and crisp on the outside but still soft on the inside. Remove them from the oil with a slotted spoon onto a paper towel. Sprinkle with desired topping.

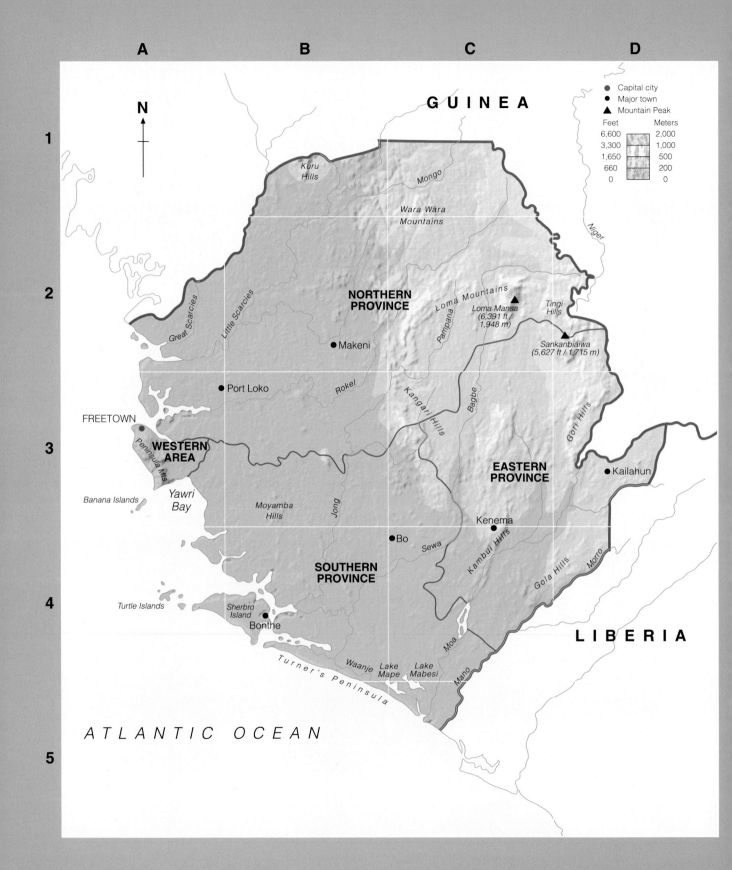

A B C D

N

1

GUINEA

Kuru
Hills

Mongo

Wara Wara
Mountains

Capital city
Major town
Mountain Peak

Feet   Meters
6,600   2,000
3,300   1,000
1,650   500
660   200
0   0

2

NORTHERN
PROVINCE

Loma Mountains

Loma Mansa ▲
(6,391 ft /
1,948 m)

Tingi
Hills

Sankanbiaiwa ▲
(5,627 ft / 1,715 m)

Great Scarcies

Little Scarcies

Pampana

● Makeni

Niger

3

FREETOWN

WESTERN
AREA

Peninsula Mts.

Yawri
Bay

Banana Islands

● Port Loko

Rokel

Kangari Hills

Bagbe

Gori Hills

EASTERN
PROVINCE

● Kailahun

Moyamba
Hills

Jong

Kenema

4

Turtle Islands

Sherbro
Island

● Bonthe

SOUTHERN
PROVINCE

●Bo

Sewa

Kambui Hills

Gola Hills

Morro

Moa

LIBERIA

Turner's Peninsula

Waanje

Lake
Mape

Lake
Mabesi

Mano

ATLANTIC OCEAN

5

MAP OF SIERRA LEONE

ECONOMIC SIERRA LEONE

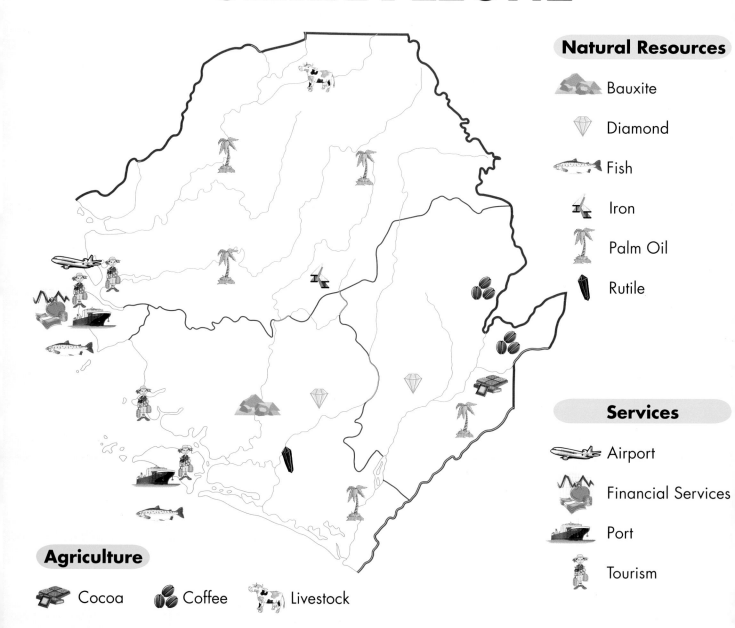

Natural Resources

- Bauxite
- Diamond
- Fish
- Iron
- Palm Oil
- Rutile

Services

- Airport
- Financial Services
- Port
- Tourism

Agriculture

- Cocoa
- Coffee
- Livestock

ABOUT THE ECONOMY

OVERVIEW

Despite having substantial mineral, agricultural, and fishery resources, Sierra Leone remains an extremely poor African nation with tremendous inequality in income distribution. Its economic and social infrastructure remain limited, and serious political disturbances continue to hinder economic development. The lack of foreign investment has stalled the government's plans to reopen the country's diamond and bauxite mines. The majority of Sierra Leoneans engage in subsistence agriculture. Some official statistics, including those concerning poverty levels and unemployment rates, have not been collected in more than a decade.

GROSS DOMESTIC PRODUCT (GDP)

$3.335 billion (2004 estimate)

GDP SECTORS

Agriculture 49 percent, industry 30 percent, services 21 percent (2001 estimate)

CURRENCY

1 Sierra Leone leone (SLL) = 100 cents
Notes: 10,000, 5,000, 2,000, 1,000, 500 leones
Coins: 100, 50 leones
1 USD = 2,350 SLL (May 2006)

ECONOMIC GROWTH RATE

6 percent (2004 estimate)

LAND AREA

27,700 square miles (71,740 square km)

AGRICULTURAL PRODUCTS

Rice, coffee, cocoa, palm kernels, palm oil, peanuts, poultry, cattle, sheep, pigs, fish

INDUSTRIAL PRODUCTS

Diamond mining, manufacturing (beverages, textiles, cigarettes, footwear), petroleum refining, small commercial ship repair

MAIN EXPORTS

Diamonds, rutile (ore of titanium), cocoa, coffee, fish (1999)

MAIN IMPORTS

Food products, machinery and equipment, fuels and lubricants, chemicals (1995)

MAJOR TRADE PARTNERS

Belgium, Germany, Cote D'Ivoire, United Kingdom, United States, China, Netherlands, South Africa

PORTS AND HARBORS

Freetown, Pepel, Sherbro Island

INTERNATIONAL AIRPORTS

Freetown (2004)

CULTURAL
SIERRA LEONE

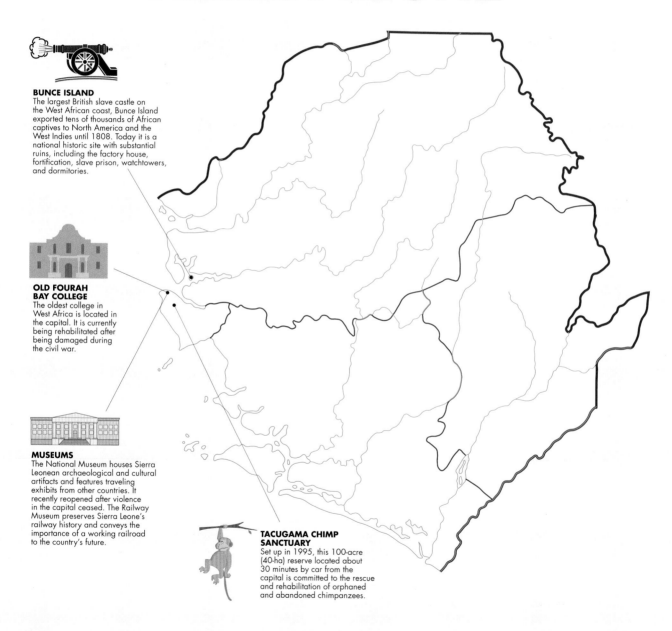

BUNCE ISLAND
The largest British slave castle on the West African coast, Bunce Island exported tens of thousands of African captives to North America and the West Indies until 1808. Today it is a national historic site with substantial ruins, including the factory house, fortification, slave prison, watchtowers, and dormitories.

OLD FOURAH BAY COLLEGE
The oldest college in West Africa is located in the capital. It is currently being rehabilitated after being damaged during the civil war.

MUSEUMS
The National Museum houses Sierra Leonean archaeological and cultural artifacts and features traveling exhibits from other countries. It recently reopened after violence in the capital ceased. The Railway Museum preserves Sierra Leone's railway history and conveys the importance of a working railroad to the country's future.

TACUGAMA CHIMP SANCTUARY
Set up in 1995, this 100-acre (40-ha) reserve located about 30 minutes by car from the capital is committed to the rescue and rehabilitation of orphaned and abandoned chimpanzees.

ABOUT
THE CULTURE

OFFICIAL NAME
Republic of Sierra Leone

CAPITAL
Freetown

OTHER IMPORTANT CITIES
Bo, Kenema, Makeni

POPULATION
6,017,643 (July 2005 estimate)

POPULATION GROWTH RATE
2.22 percent (2005 estimate)

ADMINISTRATIVE DIVISIONS
Eastern, Northern, Southern, Western

LITERACY RATE
29.6 percent (2000 estimate)

ETHNIC GROUPS
Native African 90 percent (Temne 30 percent, Mende 30 percent, other 30 percent), Krio 10 percent

MAJOR RELIGIONS
Muslim 60 percent, traditional African 30 percent, Christian 10 percent

OFFICIAL LANGUAGE
English

MAJOR HOLIDAYS
New Year's Day (January 1), Taboski (January), Good Friday, Easter, Easter Monday (March/April), Prophet Muhammad's Birthday (April 21), Independence Day (April 27), Revolution Day (April 29), Korite (date varies), Christmas Day (December 25), Boxing Day (December 26)

LEADERS IN POLITICS
Granville Sharp—founded Freetown Colony 1808
Sir Milton Margai—first prime minister (1961–64)
Sir Albert Margai—second prime minister (1964–67)
Siaka Stevens—leader of opposition party APC, prime minister, and first president (1968–85)
Foday Sankoh—leader of rebel group RUF (1990–2001)
Ahmad Kabbah—president (1996–)

137

TIME LINE

IN SIERRA LEONE	IN THE WORLD
	753 B.C. Rome is founded.
	A.D. 600 Height of Mayan civilization
	1000 The Chinese perfect gunpowder and begin to use it in warfare.
1462 Portuguese explorer Pedro da Cinta names the territory Sierra Leone (Lion Mountains).	
1495 Portuguese build a fort at Sierra Leone.	**1530** Beginning of trans-Atlantic slave trade organ- ized by the Portuguese in Africa.
1560s British ships arrive.	**1558–1603** Reign of Elizabeth I of England
	1620 Pilgrims sail the *Mayflower* to America.
1652 First slaves in North America are brought from Sierra Leone.	
1772 British acquire land from tribal leaders to repatriate slaves.	**1776** U.S. Declaration of Independence
	1789–99 The French Revolution
1808 Freetown becomes crown colony settled by freed slaves.	**1861** The U.S. Civil War begins.
	1869 The Suez Canal is opened.
1896 Britain proclaims a protectorate over the Sierra Leone mainland.	**1914** World War I begins.
1924 First election of parliamentary council under constitution.	**1939** World War II begins.
	1945 The United States drops atomic bombs on Hiroshima and Nagasaki.
1954 Sir Milton Margai appointed chief minister	**1949** The North Atlantic Treaty Organization (NATO) is formed.

IN SIERRA LEONE		IN THE WORLD
	1957	
		The Russians launch Sputnik.
1961		
Sierra Leone achieves independence.		
1967	**1966–69**	
Military coup deposes Siaka Stevens.		The Chinese Cultural Revolution
1971		
Sierra Leone is declared a republic.		
1985		
Joseph Saidu Momoh becomes president.	**1986**	
		Nuclear power disaster at Chernobyl in Ukraine
	1991	
1992		Break-up of the Soviet Union
Momoh ousted in military coup led by Valentine Strasser.		
1996		
Strasser ousted in coup led by Julius Maada Bio. Ahmad Tejan Kabbah elected president.		
1997	**1997**	
Paul Koroma deposes Kabbah, suspends the constitution and abolishes political parties.		Hong Kong is returned to China.
1998		
West African troops drive rebels out of Freetown. Kabbah makes triumphant return.		
1999		
Sankoh supporters invade Freetown.		
2000		
British paratroopers capture Sankoh.		
2001	**2001**	
Disarmament begins. British-trained Sierra Leone government forces deploy.		Terrorists crash planes in New York, Washington, D.C., and Pennsylvania.
2002		
Kabbah wins landslide election.		
2003	**2003**	
Sankoh dies while awaiting trial.		War in Iraq
2004		
War crimes trials begin. United Nations hands security in Freetown to local forces.		

GLOSSARY

AFRC
The Armed Forces Revolutionary Council, a splinter group of the Sierra Leone Army that staged a coup in 1997 and aligned itself with the Revolutionary United Front (RUF).

balangi
A musical instrument similar to a xylophone played in traditional Sierra Leonean music.

bongo
A large antelope that lives in the mountain forests of central and West Africa, including Sierra Leone.

Creoles
The descendants of freed slaves, primarily from Great Britain and the United States, who settled Freetown beginning in 1787.

ECOWAS
Economic Community of West African States, a regional group of 15 countries that attempts to lessen trade barriers and increase economic and political cooperation.

gara
Traditional woven and dyed cloth.

Gullah
Descendants of slaves from Sierra Leone and West Africa who farmed the rice plantations of South Carolina and Georgia.

Hobatoke
Sherbro creator of the universe.

Krio
First language of the Creoles and second language for most of the other residents of Sierra Leone.

kur
A Sierra Leonean stringed instrument.

nga-fa
Ancestor spirits of the Mende religion.

Ngewo
Mende creator of the universe.

nomoli
Sculptures of human figures carved out of soapstone.

NRC
National Reformation Council; the group that took over the government in 1967 and suspended the constitution.

pomtan
Sculptures of human figures carved out of wood.

protectorate
A state or territory controlled by another state.

sansa
A small pianolike instrument played with the thumb.

syllabary
A collection of characters each representing a sound or a syllable of a language.

FURTHER INFORMATION

BOOKS

Brimson, Samuel. *Nations of the World: Sierra Leone to United Arab Emirates.* Milwaukee, WI: World Almanac Library, 2003.

Campbell, Greg. *Blood Diamonds.* New York: Westview Press, 2002.

Fitzpatrick, Mary, et al. Lonely Planet. *Lonely Planet West Africa.* Melbourne: Lonely Planet, 2002.

Jackson, Michael. *In Sierra Leone.* Durham, NC: Duke University Press, 2004.

Lilly, Melinda. *Tamba and the Chief: A Temne Legend.* Jefferson City, MO: Troll Communications, 2001.

Milsome, John. *Sierra Leone.* New York: Chelsea House, 1988.

WEB SITES

All Africa: Sierra Leone. www.allafrica.com/sierraleone

Awareness Times. http://news.sl/drwebsite/publish/index.shtml

Central Intelligence Agency World Factbook (select Sierra Leone from the country list). www.cia.gov/cia/publications/factbook

Cocorioko newspaper. www.cocorioko.com

Showbiz Sierra Leone. www.showbizsierraleone.com

Sierra Leone News and Information. www.statehouse-sl.org

VIDEOS

Cry Freetown. Directed by Ron McCullagh. Insight News Television, 2000.

The Language You Cry In. Directed by Alvaro Toepke. California Showreel, 2000.

BIBLIOGRAPHY

Alie, Joe A. *A New History of Sierra Leone*. New York: St. Martin's Press, 1990.

Bergner, Daniel. *In the Land of Magic Soldiers*. New York: Farrar, Straus and Giroux, 2003.

Morgan-Conteh, Earl and Mac Dixon-Fyle. *Sierra Leone at the End of the Twentieth Century*. New York: Peter Lang Publishing, 1999.

West, Richard. *Back to Africa: A History of Sierra Leone and Liberia*. New York: Holt, Rinehart and Winston, 1970.

INDEX